PROVERBS

God's Guide for Life's Choices

Woodrow Kroll

Back to the Bible
Lincoln, Nebraska

Acknowledgments

Years ago people believed that land was power. The more land you had, the more power you had. But all that changed. After World War II, money became power. It was not how much land you owned but how much money you had that gave you power. Now the essence of power has shifted again. Instead of land or money, information has became the new power broker. The more information you have, the more power you have.

In this information age, we are now suffering from an information glut. There are just too many facts, too many things to download from computer online services, too much information for us to process effectively.

But while we have an abundance of information, we suffer from a dearth of wisdom. Many people who possess the world's information do not possess God's wisdom. Real wisdom—wisdom that comes from God—is not found in the information of our age. God's wisdom is found in the Bible, God's Word.

Proverbs: God's Guide for Life's Choices will help you discover the wisdom of God. It is a study in the Book of Proverbs, perhaps the greatest single source of God's wisdom. Here you will gain God's perspective on relationships with your neighbors, your children, your relatives and others. You will discover God's way to make and manage your money. More important, you will be guided to the right choices in life because you apply eternal wisdom to your everyday decisions.

Bringing you the wisdom of God in this book is not the work of the author alone. Back to the Bible is a team of highly dedicated men and women committed to changing lives. If reading this book changes your life, you will want to thank Allen Bean, who assisted me in research and writing, Rachel Derowitsch, who provided capable editorial assistance, and Kim Johnson, who creatively conceptualized the cover design.

Also, I express personal thanks to my friend and colleague Al Zoller, director of Publications at Back to the Bible, for leading a team of print professionals in the publication of this book.

God communicated the wisdom of Proverbs to Solomon and others. *Proverbs: God's Guide for Life's Choices* is not additional wisdom but the practical application of Proverb's wisdom to your daily life. Are you inundated by information? Then you will enjoy cutting through the information to find real wisdom.

Contents

Introduction .7

1. Wisdom and Her Relationships 13

2. Wisdom and Your Goals 27

3. Wisdom and Your Worship 35

4. Wisdom and Your Happiness 51

5. Wisdom and Your Wealth 63

6. Wisdom and Your Spouse 79

7. Wisdom and Your Children 99

8. Wisdom and Your Relatives 115

9. Wisdom and Your Friends 129

10. Wisdom and Your Purity 147

11. Wisdom and Your Words 165

12. Wisdom and Your Faith 185

13. Wisdom and Your Commitment 201

Conclusion .217

The Pursuit of Wisdom

*The LORD by wisdom founded the earth;
by understanding He established the heavens.*
Proverbs 3:19

Wisdom. Everybody wants it, but where can we find it? People search for wisdom through many avenues. The airwaves are filled with television and radio programs that allow people to express their opinions and give us their insight. Popular magazines offer advice on everything from adenoids to zippers. Bookstore shelves are crammed with "how-to" books that gross millions of dollars. If taped end-to-end, the daily newspaper advice columns written by "experts" would likely circle the equator several times. Are you surprised? You shouldn't be.

Nothing new

The proliferation of wisdom is not a new phenomenon. As Solomon said, "Of making many books there is no end" (Eccl. 12:12). Even before the Bible was written, the ancient world was filled with its own brand of wisdom. Some of it is remarkably similar to that found in the Scriptures. For example, in *The Teaching of Ptahhotep*, written around 2450 B.C., the author gives this advice when an employee dines with his employer:

> "Take what he may give, when it is set before thy nose. . . . Do not pierce him with many stares. . . . Laugh after he laughs, and it will be very pleasing to his heart."[1]

Compare this with Proverbs 23:1–2, which says, "When you sit down to eat with a ruler, consider carefully what is before you; and put a knife to your throat if you are a man given to appetite." Some scholars suggest these similarities indicate the Bible copied the secular works available at the time. That explanation, however, is unnecessary. Truth is truth, whether written 5,000 years ago, 200 years ago or yesterday. The essence of humans needs hasn't changed—and neither has the advice on how to meet our needs.

The Bible often alludes to the wise men of the nations around Israel. While maintaining that Israel's King Solomon surpassed them all, the author of 1 Kings includes a note of respect for "the wisdom of all the men of the East and all the wisdom of Egypt" (1 Kings 4:30).

Ancient wisdom books such as *The Words of Altikar* (a 7th century B.C. Assyrian sage), *The Instructions of Ani* (11th–8th century B.C.) and *The Instruction of Amenemope* (14th–11th century B.C.) often encouraged high moral standards and common sense. They warned against fraud, slander and adultery and exhorted readers to give to those in need and to discipline their children. This is evidence that God, in His common grace, did not forget those who were not part of His covenant relationship with Israel. He has loved the world from its beginning (John 3:16). Even though they rejected Him, God still gave individuals outside of His covenant sufficient understanding to attain a degree of wisdom.

Something new

All of these ancient books, however, lacked something. They lacked that special touch of God, which we call "inspiration." Divine inspiration sets the Bible apart from every other book. If we did not have the Bible, we would have human insight but no divine instruction on how to live righteously in this life or how to live eternally with God hereafter.

As a whole, God's Word contains many types of literature. Included are historical books (such as 1 & 2 Samuel and 1 & 2 Kings in the Old Testament and Acts in the New

Testament), prophetical books (Isaiah through Malachi in the Old Testament and Revelation in the New Testament) and doctrinal books (such as the letters written by Paul and Peter). All of these are a source of wisdom. Second Timothy 3:16 says, "All Scripture is given by inspiration of God, and is profitable for doctrine, for reproof, for correction, for instruction in righteousness." But there are some sections of Scripture that God has given for the express purpose of teaching the reader how to live a life pleasing to Him.

Moral wisdom

In the Old Testament, the books of Proverbs, Job, Ecclesiastes and the Song of Solomon are designated specifically as "wisdom literature."[2] Of these, Proverbs plainly declares that its purpose is "to know wisdom and instruction, to perceive the words of understanding, to receive the instruction of wisdom, justice, judgment, and equity; to give prudence to the simple, to the young man knowledge and discretion" (Prov. 1:2-4).

In other words, Solomon says that the purpose of Proverbs is twofold: (1) to help us acquire a disciplined skill in right living and (2) to help us gain the acumen to know what *is* right living.

More than ever, we need this kind of wisdom. Many people no longer have the disciplined skills or moral acumen to live wisely. According to a report from Ohio State University, many teenagers don't understand why they shouldn't steal. This study measured moral development among 323 adolescents, about half of whom were incarcerated. More than 90 percent of these young people said stealing is wrong. But the most common reason for not sealing was that "you might get caught and punished." Other reasons included "the other person might get even" and "you might not need the item."

A more mature perspective would understand that stealing is wrong because it hurts other people and damages society as a whole by destroying the sense of communal trust.[3] Without this kind of wisdom and growing maturity, the future looks bleak indeed.

Supernatural wisdom

As we have seen, however, moral wisdom is not what sets the Bible's wisdom apart from other forms of wisdom. What makes the wisdom of the Word so unique is it possesses a supernatural power. It is not only the truth of God, but the Bible has the ability to help the reader to apply its truth through the power of the Holy Spirit. Distinguished theologian F. F. Bruce noted, "The word of human beings, however wise in substance or eloquent in expression, cannot produce spiritual life; this is the prerogative of the Word of God."

As confirmation of its supernatural character, the Bible claims to come directly from God (the word *inspiration* in 2 Timothy 3:16 literally means "God breathed out"). No one knows how to organize and direct our lives better than the One who created us.

Once when I was preaching in Lancaster County, Pennsylvania, an older gentleman in the congregation volunteered to escort me to the many interesting sites of Amish country. We went to an Amish farm, now a tourist site. As the guide took a group of us through the house, my friend would add little tidbits about each room, such as, "This used to be two rooms," or, "The sink was originally over there." I didn't think much about it, and neither did the guide, until the man whispered to me, "My bed used to be in that corner." I looked at him in amazement. My elderly friend had grown up in that house. It was his home for many years, and he had made the renovations the guide was talking about. I had been listening to a trained guide when the creator was at my side.

Many men have written great books. Every era has been blessed with authors such as Homer, Shakespeare, Milton and Dickens. But only The Book can legitimately claim to make great men. The Bible is not the work of a trained guide; it alone is the wisdom of the Creator.

How the advice is given

When we think of wisdom, often our minds conjure up memories of long sermons by the pastor or lectures from our parents. But Proverbs is not like that. It dishes up its wisdom in the form of short, pithy statements. The writers used several literary forms to make their words of wisdom more memorable:

Synonymous parallelism. The writer says a line and then repeats the same line in similar form. For example, "Pride goes before destruction, / And a haughty spirit before a fall" (Prov. 16:18). "O you simple ones, understand prudence, / And you fools, be of an understanding heart" (8:5). No new information is added in the second line; it simply reiterates the first for emphasis.

Antithetic parallelism. In this form, the writer makes a statement and then contrasts it with a second statement. For example, "A wise son makes a glad father, / But a foolish son is the grief of his mother" (10:1). "A merry heart does good, like medicine, / But a broken spirit dries the bones" (17:22). In essence, it's like looking at both sides of the same coin. The contrast helps us remember the lesson to be learned.

Synthetic parallelism. In this third form, the writer simply continues the thought of the first line. For example, "In the fear of the LORD there is strong confidence, / And His children will have a place of refuge" (14:26). "Give instruction to a wise man, and he will be still wiser; / Teach a just man, and he will increase in learning" (9:9). In these instances the material is expanded upon to give a fuller understanding.

The choice is yours

A lot of people are ready to give us advice. There is no shortage of talk these days. But how can you be sure what you read and hear is true? There's only one way. Compare the wisdom around you with God's eternal and timeless wisdom. That means you have to come back to the Bible. You must choose whether you want to listen to a guide who has learned a few facts or to the divine Creator. If you want to listen to the Creator, you have no better source than God's Word and no better place to find His practical wisdom than the Book of Proverbs.

God's wisdom is real wisdom. It is not flawed as is the wisdom of man. It is pure wisdom from heaven. It will lead you back to Him and teach you how to make the right choices in life. If making right choices is important to you, choices that bring good to you and glory to God, the Book of Proverbs is the place to look.

---

[1] Derek Kidner, *Proverbs* (London: InterVarsity Press, 1973), p. 19.

[2] Some scholars include the Book of Psalms, but the wisdom there tends to be of a slightly different nature than in the other four books.

[3] *National & International Religion Report*, April 3, 1995, p. 8.

Chapter 1

Wisdom and Her Relationships

A wise man will hear and increase learning.
Proverbs 1:5

A sign on a school bulletin board read: "Free wisdom Monday through Friday. Bring your own container." That same sign is appropriate for the Book of Proverbs too. God's wisdom is free to us, anytime day or night, but we need to know where to find it. Proverbs was written to give us wisdom from God in making many of the tough choices we face in life. Proverb 1:5 says, "Let the wise listen and add to their learning" (NIV). That's good advice for everyone!

Worldly wisdom is foolishness

Few people consider themselves foolish; nevertheless, when it comes to God and eternal matters we often are. Popular opinion cannot be trusted to always hold true. For example, Thomas Watson, chairman of IBM, said in 1943, "I think there is a world market for about five computers." Ken Olson, president of Digital Equipment Corporation, said in 1977, "There is no reason for any individual to have a computer in their home." History has shown this worldly wisdom to be folly on a grand scale!

Fuzzy thinking

When we try to understand God with human reasoning, our thinking gets fuzzy. We have some blind spots that cause us to miss vital insights.

We're a little like one of the passengers on a four-engine airplane. The pilot came on the intercom and announced that one of the engines on the left side of the plane had failed. "Don't be alarmed," he said. "We can still make it to our destination on three engines, but we'll probably arrive about fifteen minutes late."

A few moments later the pilot came back on the intercom. "Those on the right side of the plane may be aware that a second engine has failed. Don't be concerned. We can make it to our destination on two engines, but we'll likely be thirty minutes late."

Soon the pilot made another announcement. "It has just come to my attention that a third engine has failed. Don't be alarmed. We can still fly with just one engine. Unfortunately, we'll be about forty-five minutes late."

The passenger turned to the man next to him and said, "I hope that fourth engine doesn't fail or we could be up here all night."

Erroneous thinking

Most human wisdom doesn't function quite as erroneous as this, but in regard to eternal issues— those things that pertain to God— this is often how many men and women think. It is estimated that 12 million people in the United States believe that flaming balls of gas located light years from our planet control their destinies. These people keep 175,000 part-time and 10,000 full-time astrologers busy in the United States. Great Britain even has diploma-issuing colleges for astrologers, with ever-increasing enrollments. When it comes to thinking about God and the supernatural, something happens to the reasoning powers of otherwise intelligent people.

Natural thinking

Admittedly, foolishness is a natural part of man. Proverbs 22:15 reminds us, "Foolishness is bound up in the heart of a child, but the rod of correction will drive it far from him." We are born with an innate waywardness. That's why it is so important that we find a wisdom beyond what the world can offer.

Secular wisdom is knowledge

The academic world looks with disdain upon the foolishness of worldly wisdom. In their pursuit of knowledge, academicians claim to find no place for unscientific opinions. They deal only with the "facts." Yet these men and women are deluged by the sheer volume of knowledge. Information today is increasing at a mind-boggling rate. If we were to convert knowledge into feet and inches, man's accumulated knowledge from the beginning of recorded history to 1845 would represent one inch; what he learned from 1845 until 1945 would amount to three inches; and what he learned from 1945 until 1975 would represent the height of the Washington Monument. Since 1975, knowledge has at least doubled. No one can possibly stay on top of this much information.

Knowledge without understanding

In an essay on literature and technology, literary critic Cleanth Brooks observed, "Secretly we may hunger for wisdom, but our overt craving nowadays is, of course, for information." Later in this article, Brooks mentions the famous lines from T. S. Eliot that lament the loss of wisdom in the growing flood of public knowledge, and the loss even of knowledge in a deluge of sheer information.[1]

While no one would deny that knowledge is on the rise at a record-breaking pace, few people would argue that wisdom has kept abreast. If anything, man's understanding of what is right or wrong in what he does has decreased as his knowledge has increased. Some years ago Max Bonn, a nuclear physicist and a close friend of Albert Einstein, was interviewed on German television. In response to a question from the interviewer, he made this wise observation, "I'd be happier if we had scientists with less brains and more wisdom."

Knowledge without backbone

Knowledge is simply the accumulation of facts, and unlike wisdom, it does not have the ability to supply the moral backbone to do what needs to be done. For example, economists have confirmed for years the serious financial state of our nation. The facts are in. But politicians responsible to handle this problem refuse to risk the negative backlash that may occur if they do something about it.

Scientists also have documented the worsening of the ozone layer around our planet, but again those who are responsible for making decisions that could change the situation are reluctant to take the necessary steps. Many people have knowledge but not the moral courage to implement it.

Knowledge without morals

Furthermore, an accumulation of facts does not guarantee that we will use those facts in a beneficial way. For example, we have the knowledge necessary to create very powerful explosives. This knowledge allows us to build roads through terrain that otherwise would have been impossible to build. It enables demolition experts to bring down multi-storied buildings in a matter of seconds with incredible precision. Yet that same knowledge was used to destroy the Oklahoma City Federal Building in 1995, killing 168 people and injuring 500 others.

Knowledge represents a disaster waiting to happen. It is at the mercy of its user. By itself, knowledge lacks both the resolve and the ability to be appropriately applied. Because that resolve is absent, knowledge cannot guarantee by itself that it will always be used to heal rather than hurt, to build up rather than tear down, to move man toward God rather than away from Him.

Without divine wisdom, knowledge is dangerous. Those bogged down in secular wisdom could indeed fit the definition of *sophomore*, which literally means "wise fools" (Greek: *sophos*—wise, *moros*—fool). By tenth grade many young people have learned a little but are convinced they know it all. Likewise, the wise men of this world have gathered a few facts but are convinced they have the answer to everything. They don't.

Biblical wisdom is reality

One of the accusations leveled against Christians is that they cannot face reality so they retreat into their religion. A thoughtful consideration of the facts, however, shows the opposite is true.

Worldly wisdom is inadequate

Worldly wisdom tries to ignore reality. Its philosophy is "eat, drink and be merry—because if we deny unpleasant truths long enough, maybe they will go away." This is the philosophy that fuels our mad passion for distractions. Why else do we treat sports heroes like gods when many have acted like fools? Why else do we constantly need the pounding of a boom box or a Walkman® in our ears? Why else do we flock to entertainment events by the thousands? Could it be we fear that in silence and solitude we might come face to face with reality? *Escapism* is the watch word of worldly wisdom. Go to Disney World, attend a rock concert, get high on drugs—but by no means let the realities of life intrude upon your consciousness.

Secular wisdom is inadequate

Secular wisdom, on the other hand, may face reality but it doesn't know what to do with it. It collects the facts, but then what? It's like having an angry tiger by the tail—you don't know what to do with it but you don't dare let go.

Biblical wisdom is the only form of wisdom that faces reality with the understanding and motivation to do something about it. Who built the first hospitals? Christians did, because they faced the reality that people get hurt and sick. Biblical wisdom says we are responsible to care for those who need help physically and emotionally as well as spiritually. Who founded the first orphanage? Christians did, because they faced the reality that parents sometimes die before their children are grown. Biblical wisdom says we are to care for the fatherless. Committed Christians have proven over and over again that with God's guidance they are able to confront reality and make it better.

God's wisdom is the answer

Biblical wisdom is not escapism nor a mere collection of facts. It is reality in coveralls. It is Truth with dirt under her fingernails. We need biblical wisdom in the marketplace—and that is the wisdom addressed in the Book of Proverbs.

Proverbs wisdom

A special repository of biblical wisdom is found in the Book of Proverbs. This book gets its name from the opening noun, *misle*. This word, which we translate as "proverbs," comes from a Hebrew verb meaning "to be like, to be compared with, to be parallel, to be similar."[2] Jews used proverbs to help their young people learn skills in living. By using comparisons, contrasts and similes, the writer encouraged his readers to think more closely about what was being said. The proverb became a matter to "chew on" or meditate upon until every last ounce of wisdom was extracted.

Consequently, Proverbs demonstrates a wisdom that is:

a. Practical. The theme of wisdom runs throughout the 31 chapters of Proverbs. The primary word in the Old Testament for wisdom is *hokmah*. It was frequently used to describe the skill of craftsmen. When the need for clothing for the priests arose, God told Moses, "So you shall speak to all who are gifted artisans, whom I have filled with the spirit of *wisdom*, that they may make Aaron's garments, to sanctify him, that he may minister to Me as priest" (Ex. 28:3, italics mine). The special skill needed to create the garments for the high priest was designated as a gift of wisdom.

Proverbs wisdom is not confined to an ivory tower. It has no interest in settling the intricate questions of theology that have kept both amateur and professional theologians busy for centuries. Instead, this wisdom encourages a form of piety that is as much at home in the workplace, at school or on the golf course as it is at church.

For example, Proverbs tells us, "Do not devise evil against your neighbor, for he dwells by you for safety's sake" (3:29). Again we are told, "As iron sharpens iron, so a man sharpens the countenance of his friend" (27:17). That is practical wisdom, wisdom that will help us make right choices in life.

This does not mean that morality is sacrificed on the altar of practicality. In some churches today we find an "if it works, do it" mentality— but not in Proverbs. Certainly, morality and practicality often run side by side. The most practical approach one can have is the attitude that says, "God knows how to do this best; therefore I will do it His way." On those occasions where morality and practicality appear to part company, there is no doubt which one we are to follow— morality. For example, Proverbs 18:16 says, "A man's gift makes room for him, and brings him before great men." But Proverbs also says, "A wicked man accepts a bribe behind the back to pervert the ways of justice" (17:23). Do what is practical, unless what is practical conflicts with what is moral.

The wisdom of Proverbs is pragmatic, but it is not an "anything goes" approach. Those who never leave their homes may not need this kind wisdom. The rest of us do!

b. Godly. Biblical wisdom always sees the wicked man as a fool and the godly man as wise. Proverbs says, "He who is quick-tempered acts foolishly, and a man of wicked intentions is hated" (14:7). And again, "If the righteous will be recompensed on the earth, how much more the ungodly and the sinner" (11:31). Also, "A good man obtains favor from the LORD, but a man of wicked intentions He will condemn. A man is not established by wickedness, but the root of the righteous cannot be moved" (12:2–3).

In Proverbs it is understood that one cannot be wise unless one is also good. A good man is obedient to God and His standards. God, as our Creator, established boundaries for our protection. Only a fool would cross them.

In early 1988 Charles and Diana, Prince and Princess of Wales, were on a skiing trip to Switzerland along with some friends. One afternoon an avalanche caused a terrible accident in which one of the prince's lifelong friends was killed and another seriously injured. A day or two later the press reported that the prince's group had chosen to ski on slopes that were closed to the public. Avalanche warnings were posted but ignored. The prince's party chose to go beyond the fences because, as one of them observed, that's where the optimum fun and excitement were to be found. The price tag for such fun was extremely high.

This is one of the primary lessons of Proverbs: When faced with life's choices, stay within God's boundaries. Only a fool would risk the consequences of straying outside them.

c. Intimate. In the 31 chapters of Proverbs, God's name is used approximately 100 times. In all but a dozen instances the name used is the covenant name *Yahweh.* This implies a special, intimate, covenant relationship with God. Proverbs does not record a wisdom for everyone. While unbelievers could benefit from some of its advice, the real counsel in the Book of Proverbs is for the person who has a personal relationship with God. The teaching of Proverbs is that biblical wisdom fosters intimacy between God and man. The person who wants to know God better needs to know and apply the wisdom in the Book of Proverbs.

Man's blindness

Sadly, man is usually blind to his need for wisdom other than his own. His heart naturally rebels against God. In the

New International Version Proverbs 19:3 says, "A man's own folly ruins his life, yet his heart *rages* against the LORD" (italics mine). Most people foolishly are so convinced their way is the right way that they don't know how wrong they are. Proverbs 14:12 warns, "There is a way which seems right to a man, but its end is the way of death."

The word *death* can mean spiritual death (as in Genesis 2:17) or physical death. Every human being is spiritually dead at physical birth (Eph. 2:1). In essence, we are still-born spiritually. Pursuing our own wisdom, wisdom that separates us from God and seals our future without Him, is the ultimate evidence of the blindness of our hearts and lack of spiritual life.

Spiritual separation

As man's knowledge has increased, so has his spiritual estrangement from God. Our human knowledge often carves a deeper chasm between God and us. For example, using the Internet you can now communicate with people all over the world, but it's also possible to access pornographic literature that once was available only in adult bookstores. Chat rooms— places where computer users can meet on-line and discuss a variety of topics— have been used by perverted people to make contact with impressionable children for soliciting sex. One teenage boy received a plane ticket to fly from the Midwest to California to meet an older man. In this instance the police were able to locate him and bring him home. Others are not so fortunate.

Sooner or later spiritual death leads to physical death. If we engage in activities that are contrary to God's will we jeopardize our lives. Alcohol- and drug-related deaths, AIDS and lung cancer, for instance, may not be God's punishment for engaging in sinful behavior, but they are the natural consequences of failing to follow His wisdom. God hates sin because it hurts what He loves the most— human beings.

Damage control

God's wisdom is geared to helping us avoid the damage sin will do to our lives. Blindness to His wisdom increases the chances of harming ourselves. Proverbs says, "But the path of the just is like the shining sun, that shines ever brighter unto the perfect day. The way of the wicked is like darkness; they do not know what makes them stumble" (4:18–19). Picture someone walking through a minefield in the middle of the night without a map, and you have an idea of what the writer of Proverbs means.

The world is a dangerous place, full of booby traps and pitfalls. It is even more dangerous if you walk through it with your eyes closed. But you don't have to. The Book of Proverbs will help you open your eyes and make the right choices in the minefield of life.

God's solution

God has an incredible love for every one of us. Out of that love He has provided a way for us to have access to His wisdom. It begins with salvation. The writer of Proverbs says, "Love covers all sins" (10:12). Again, "He who covers a transgression seeks love, but he who repeats a matter separates friends" (17:9). When we receive Jesus Christ as our Savior, His blood covers our sin. But that blood flows from a heart of love. We are saved not by our own merit but because God loved us and gave us His Son to redeem us from our sins (John 3:16; Acts 20:28; 1 Cor. 6:20).

At the time of our salvation, the Holy Spirit comes to dwell in our lives (Acts 1:5). God's Spirit supernaturally illumines our minds so we can understand His Word (1 John 2:27). Without that illumination, the Bible seems like foolishness (1 Cor. 1:21-23). But with the Spirit as our teacher (John 14:26), all Scripture becomes "profitable for doctrine, for reproof, for correction, for instruction in righteousness" (2 Tim. 3:16). The Bible is understandable if we have the help of the right teacher.

God's instrument

God used three men to pass on His wisdom in the Book of Proverbs. Two of them, Agur and Lemuel[3], may not have been Jewish (these are not Jewish names). But God used Solomon, David's son by Bathsheba, as His instrument to convey the majority of the wisdom found in this book. Three thousand proverbs are ascribed to Solomon, as well as 1,005 songs (1 Kings 4:32).

Solomon requested an "understanding heart" (or a "heart of wisdom") shortly after becoming king of Israel (1 Kings 3:4-15). He knew he would be called upon to make decisions that affected the lives of thousands of his people, and he was keenly aware of how inadequate his own wisdom was. That God graciously and abundantly answered Solomon's request is evident by 1 Kings 4:29-34:

> And God gave Solomon wisdom and exceedingly great understanding, and largeness of heart like the sand on the seashore. Thus Solomon's wisdom excelled the wisdom of all the men of the East and all the wisdom of Egypt. For he was wiser than all men . . . He spoke three thousand proverbs, and his songs were one thousand and five. . . . And men of all nations, from all the kings of the earth who had heard of his wisdom, came to hear the wisdom of Solomon.

There were other sources of wisdom; there were other wise men; but none could come close to the wisdom God gave Solomon. It was not that he had an unusual IQ or was holier than anyone else. This wisdom was given because Solomon asked for it. James says the same is true for us: "If any of you lacks wisdom, let him ask of God, who gives to all liberally and without reproach, and it will be given to him" (James 1:5). If you ask God to give you His wisdom in making right choices in life, He will do it.

Man's response

Life is challenging. We face questions that have life-changing consequences: What goals should I establish for my life? How can I find happiness? Where should my family come in my list of priorities? How can I get along with people on the job? How do I manage my money? What kind of person should I marry? We need God's wisdom from the Book of Proverbs to answer the myriad of questions about decisions we face daily. Unfortunately, many people— even Christians— make life's choices without the benefit of God's wisdom, and the result is often disastrous.

Before you begin reading the rest of this book, consider the following three steps:

1. If you do not have a personal relationship with Jesus Christ, ask Him to be your Savior now. Salvation is not just head knowledge; it is a personal surrender to Christ's saving grace and lordship (Acts 16:31). Without this basic step, what you read in the Book of Proverbs will seem to be foolishness. If you are not sure you have ever trusted Jesus as your Savior and are born again, pray this simple prayer:

Lord Jesus, I'm not sure if I have ever sincerely asked You to come into my life and save me. If not, I do so now. I thank You for dying on the cross for my sins. I believe that only You can save me from my sin, and I thank You for restoring my relationship with God the Father. Amen.

2. If you have a right relationship with God, confess any known sin in your life. Sin clogs the prayer line between ourselves and God. First John 1:9 says, "If we confess our sins, He is faithful and just to forgive us our sins and to cleanse us from all unrighteousness." God cannot hear your prayer for wisdom if you need forgiveness. The first act of wisdom He would have you perform is to avail yourself of the cleansing blood of Christ.

3. Finally, ask God to give you insight as you read the rest of this book and study the Book of Proverbs. Only the Holy

Spirit can illumine your mind with the understanding you need to confront the issues you face. The real teacher is the Holy Spirit. Ask Him to teach you. This book is just the Teacher's aide.

If you have followed these three steps, you are ready to explore God's wisdom. Reach out in faith and trust to the God who loves you, the One who has covered your sins with the blood of His Son, and who has a brilliant future planned for you if you follow the wisdom of His Word.

God's wisdom is free. It's available to you. Bring your own container.

---

[1] Ken Myers, "Waiting for Wisdom," *Signs of the Times*, nd., n.p., p. 58.

[2] *Theological Wordbook of the Old Testament, Vol. 1*, edited by R. Laird Harris, Gleason L. Archer Jr., and Bruce K. Waltke (Chicago: Moody Press, 1980), p. 533.

[3] Some have suggested Lemuel is the pen name for Solomon.

Chapter 2

Wisdom and Your Goals

Whoever finds me finds life.
Proverbs 8:35

Goals are important. Charlie Brown illustrates this truth in one of his infamous baseball games. Having struck out again, he reaches the depths of defeat. "Rats," he says. "I'll never be a big-league player. All my life I've dreamed of playing in the big leagues, but I don't have what it takes." Lucy tries to console him with a bit of sage advice: "Charlie Brown, you're thinking too far ahead. What you need are some intermediate goals." "Intermediate goals?" Charlie asks. "Yes," Lucy says. "Start by seeing if you can walk off the mound without falling down!"

Whether we are conscious of it or not, almost everyone has goals. For some people, their goal in life is to graduate from college and get a good job. Others want to make a ton of money— and then spend it all. Yet others have their sights set on being a powerful politician, maybe even the president of the United States.

No matter what important goals we have, God has an even bigger one. His was conceived in eternity past and will last for eternity future. God calls His goal "life." In the New Testament Jesus says, "I have come that they may have life, and that they may have it more abundantly" (John 10:10). Christ's abundant life is the most exciting adventure we can undertake, and wisdom is the key to experiencing it to the fullest. The Book of Proverbs is written to help us understand God's goal and to develop in us a wise, skillful approach to living in order that we might reach it.

The promise of wisdom

A common theme that runs through the Book of Proverbs is the promise that those who seek and find wisdom also will find life. Proverbs 8:35 says, "For whoever finds me finds life, and obtains favor from the LORD."

But there is a negative side to this truth as well. Verse 36 says, "But he who sins against me wrongs his own soul; all those who hate me love death." The word *hate* in this verse means to "love less" (as it does in Malachi 1:3 and Romans 9:13). Many people end up loving the world and the friendship of the world more than they love the wisdom God has to offer. The consequences are tragic.

So much of the foolishness and heartache we see results from the rejection of the wisdom God offers. The theory of evolution is an example. Charles Darwin's evaluation of his own theory was negative. Before his book *The Origin of Species* was published, he forewarned a friend:

> You will be greatly disappointed [by the forthcoming book]; it will be grievously too hypothetical. It will very likely be of no other service than collecting some facts; though I myself think I see my way approximately on the origin of the species. But, alas, how frequent, how almost universal it is in an author to persuade himself of the truth of his own dogmas.[1]

Yet those eager to find an alternative to the wisdom of God quickly embraced it. In the face of human logic, they pushed the acceptance of this theory so that it is now taught as fact in most academic institutions even though it defies the basic tenets of science itself. Someone suggested that the chance of higher life forms emerging through an evolutionary process is comparable to the chance that a tornado sweeping through a junkyard might assemble a Boeing 747. While it may not make sense to push such an untenable proposition as evolution, the alternative would be to accept creationism by an Almighty God. This is even more unacceptable to them.

The foolishness of man's wisdom, however, does more than deceive generations of students; it devalues life. If we are only the result of the fortuitous combination of certain chemicals joined by a freak infusion of random energy, what's our purpose? If we are merely globs of protoplasm here by chance, what difference does it make if we are aborted before we are born or terminated at the end of our usefulness? What do we have to live for?

Sociologists bemoan the increase of violence. They publish statistics such as:

• The homicide rate for males between the ages of 15 and 24 is 22 homicides per 100,000 for the United States, more than four times higher than the next highest country.

• Homicide is the most likely cause of death for young males and accounts for 42 percent of all black male deaths.

• The youth arrest rate for murder, manslaughter, rape, robbery and aggravated assault increased 16 percent between 1989 and 1990. The cost of incarcerating young offenders runs about $29,600 per person, or $1.7 billion a year.

• Seven percent of the youths account for 79 percent of all youth-committed serious, violent offenses.

• A total of $4.2 billion a year is spent on 260 delinquency prevention programs, which are spread among 17 agencies within seven federal departments.[2]

Few people make the connection between the increase of random and senseless violence and the teaching that we are the product of a random and senseless act of nature. Truly, those who reject wisdom "love death."

What is life?

But this chaotic and violent condition is far from what God wants for us. Through His wisdom, He offers us an opportunity to know life in a fashion we have never experienced before.

A Roman soldier came before Caesar to ask permission to commit suicide. Caesar looked at the wretched, dispirited man and asked, "Soldier, were you ever alive?" Obviously, Caesar and the soldier were operating on different understandings of what life is. The soldier thought only of the duration of his life, while Caesar contemplated the quality of the man's life.

Wisdom does promise longevity to our lives. Solomon says, "My son, do not forget my law, but let your heart keep my commands; for length of days and long life and peace they will add to you" (Prov. 3:1-2). Again in Proverbs 4:10 he says, "Hear, my son, and receive my sayings, and the years of your life will be many."

In the earthly sense, this is not a blanket promise. We all know godly Christians who died before they reached what we would consider a long life. Nevertheless, obedience to God's wisdom can keep us from vices and activities that would shorten our lives. For example, the Associated Press observed that life expectancy for men in New York City has declined. For the first time in the almost 100 years since records have been kept, life expectancy has decreased from 68.9 to 68.8 years. The state health department suspects the cause is AIDS, which has resulted in the death of more than 30,000 men in that city.[3] As we read these tragic figures, we must keep in mind that behind the disease is a lifestyle that is contrary to God's wisdom.

But when the Bible uses the word *life*, it includes quality as well as quantity. Without quality of life, heaven would be like hell. Greek mythology tells of a man, Timotheous, who asked the gods for eternal life, which they granted. He forgot, however, to ask for eternal youth to go with it.

Consequently, he was condemned to live forever as an aged person even though he begged for release.

No such division is found in God's definition of life. Wisdom promises a life that will not only go on eternally, but with a quality unmatched by anything the world has to offer. The essence of this quality is a relationship with God. Derek Kidner writes, "In several places it is not too much to say that 'life' means fellowship with God. Some of the major Old Testament expressions for godliness are interchangeable with 'life' or 'to live.'"[4]

A relationship with God will radically change our lives. For one thing, we experience true acceptance from Someone who knows all about us. The latter part of Proverbs 8:35 says, "and obtains favor from the LORD." The Hebrew word translated as "favor" (*ratsown*) also means "to be pleased with or accepted." Many people struggle with the feeling that "if others really knew me, they wouldn't like me." Even talented, celebrated professionals have confessed to wondering when their inadequacies would be exposed and their lives come tumbling down around their ears.

No such fears need to exist with God. He *does* know all about us. Our hearts and our lives are an open book to Him. God willingly accepts us where we are and then gradually leads us to where He knows we need to be.

On May 2, 1888, G. Campbell Morgan preached a trial sermon with the hopes of entering the Methodist ministry. Due to a set of unfortunate circumstances, he failed miserably and was rejected. Saddened, he wired his father back home just one word, "Rejected." His father wired back, "Rejected on earth, accepted in heaven." Taking that message to heart, Morgan went on to become a world-famous preacher.

Most of us like to be accepted by our family, our peers and our employers. But most important is acceptance by God. When we follow the wisdom of Proverbs, our lives will be pleasing and acceptable to Him.

God's will

The goal of life that God offers to us also ties closely to His will. True life is lived within the context of God's will. Fulfillment, peace and a sense of purpose can be found only in the heart of a person seeking to know and do the will of God. Someone rightly observed that the greatest way to live life is to find out which way God is going and go with Him. That requires us to stay in tune with His wisdom.

A former park ranger at Yellowstone National Park told of a fellow ranger who was leading a group of tourists on a hike to a fire lookout. Not wanting his explanation of the beauties around him interrupted, the ranger turned off his two-way radio. It wasn't until they nearly arrived at the lookout that they were met by another ranger. The man was almost out of breath, but when he could finally speak, he asked why no one had responded to his messages on the radio. A grizzly bear had been seen stalking the group, he said, and he was trying to warn them of the danger.

We also can't risk being out of communication with God. Satan is a predatory animal seeking whom he might destroy (1 Pet. 5:8). Having failed to prevent our defection from his kingdom (Col. 1:13), Satan tries to keep us from experiencing the abundant life. When we cut ourselves off from God's Word, we become vulnerable to Satan's attack. God's will is designed not to fence us in but to fence Satan out.

With utmost care, God communicates His wisdom to keep us safe from the clutches of this merciless and ruthless adversary. The phrase from a song popular many years ago, "fools rush in where angels fear to tread," is only too true. The moment we step out of God's will we step into Satan's way. We become vulnerable to his attack. One evening in the arms of the wrong person, or one weekend at the wrong place is all Satan needs to destroy your life.

Only the will of God offers us the opportunity to live life to the fullest. Some anonymous poet wrote:

To know God's will is life's greatest treasure. To do God's will is life's greatest pleasure.[5]

Get a life

A mother shared that her son had told her firmly but kindly, "Mom, you need to get a life." Maybe someone has expressed the same thing to you. Obviously, they are not talking about a physical life— it would be pointless to offer this advice to a corpse. Instead, they're referring to a life with quality.

God, too, desires for us to "get a life." His goal is for us to experience a life that not only lasts forever but has a quality that exceeds anything we can imagine (1 Cor. 2:9). The wisdom from Proverbs can help us receive this kind of life.

---

[1] Charles Darwin, 1858, in a letter to a colleague regarding his *Origin of Species*, as quoted in "John Lofton's Journal," the *Washington Times*, February 8, 1984.

[2] Senate Governmental Affairs Committee, General Accounting Office, reported in the *Columbus Dispatch*, April 1, 1992, p. 3A.

[3] Associated Press, January 20, 1994, via Compuserve.

[4] Kidner, *Proverbs* (London: InterVarsity Press, 1973), p. 54.

[5] *Discovery Digest*, January/February, 1983, p. 32.

Chapter 3

Wisdom and Your Worship

Do not let your heart envy sinners,
but in the fear of the LORD continue all day long.
Proverbs 23:17

In his book *Whatever Happened to Worship,* A. W. Tozer wrote,

Christian churches have come to the dangerous time predicted long ago. It is a time when we can pat one another on the back, congratulate ourselves and join in the glad refrain, "We are rich, and increased with goods, and have need of nothing!" It certainly is true that hardly anything is missing from our churches these days—except the most important thing. We are missing the genuine and sacred offering of ourselves and our worship to the God and Father of our Lord Jesus Christ.[1]

The importance of worship

Anywhere worship is absent in our churches it is a tragic loss. When we place our faith in Christ, worship becomes a necessity, not an option. As Tozer said, "We are called to an everlasting preoccupation with God." Nothing greater can fill our hearts and minds than the work and character of the Father, Son and Holy Spirit.

God expects our worship

Two assumptions run throughout Scripture. One is that man *will* worship. He may worship a rock or a tree or even himself, but he will worship something. The second assumption is that the Living God, the Holy Trinity, the great "I AM," is the only appropriate focus for our worship. God's first commandment to Moses concerned worship. He said, "You shall have no other gods before Me. You shall not make for yourself any carved image . . . For I, the LORD your God, am a jealous God, visiting the iniquity of the fathers on the children to the third and fourth generations of those who hate Me" (Ex. 20:3-5). God knew His people would worship, so that was not His concern. But He expected them to worship Him rather than false gods.

Elsewhere God says, "And it shall come to pass that from one New Moon to another, and from one Sabbath to another, all flesh shall come to worship before Me" (Isa. 66:23). Again, God expects His people to worship Him. Even the angels are expected to worship God. The writer of Hebrews indicates that the angels in heaven worship Christ (Heb. 1:6). The apostle John gives us a glimpse into a heavenly worship service in Revelation 5:

> 11 Then I looked, and I heard the voice of many angels around the throne, the living creatures, and the elders; and the number of them was ten thousand times ten thousand, and thousands of thousands,

> 12 saying with a loud voice: "Worthy is the Lamb who was slain to receive power and riches and wisdom, and strength and honor and glory and blessing!"

> 13 And every creature which is in heaven and on the earth and under the earth and such as are in the sea, and all that are in them, I heard saying: "Blessing and honor and glory and power be to Him who sits on the throne, and to the Lamb, forever and ever!"

> 14 Then the four living creatures said, "Amen!" And the twenty-four elders fell down and worshiped Him who lives forever and ever.

Worship is natural. Whether men or angels, we are created with the need to worship. God made us to worship Him.

When we worship anything less than God (and everything else is less), we cheat ourselves—and God.

Scripture commands our worship

But worship is more than a simple expectation. David says, "Give to the LORD the glory due His name; bring an offering, and come before Him. Oh, worship the LORD in the beauty of holiness!" (1 Chron. 16:29). This is a command, not a suggestion.

God wants the best for us. He wants what will bring the greatest sense of fulfillment to our lives. He wants us to focus on that which brings peace and joy to our souls. That's why He commands us to worship Him. The psalmist says, "My soul shall be satisfied as with marrow and fatness, and my mouth shall praise You with joyful lips. When I remember You on my bed, I meditate on You in the night watches" (Ps. 63:5–6).

If all who inhabit the earth are expected to worship God, and all who inhabit heaven rejoice in worshiping Him, worship must be important. We should take it seriously.

The definition

The key to this important and necessary experience of worship rests in what the Book of Proverbs calls "fear." Numerous verses in the Bible tell us to "fear the Lord." But what does that mean? The Hebrew word for *fear* is *yare*. It can mean:

1. Dread. This implies an extreme uneasiness in the face of a disagreeable prospect. It is a present feeling related to a future event. For example, David's dying charge to Solomon included this thought: "Then you will prosper, if you take care to fulfill the statutes and judgments with which the LORD charged Moses concerning Israel. Be strong and of good courage; do not *fear* nor be dismayed" (1 Chron. 22:13, italics mine).

Solomon was in a potentially dangerous situation. Whenever a transfer of power took place, the chance for a coup increased dramatically. In fact, 1 Kings 2 records the efforts of Solomon's older brother, Adonijah, to plot just such an insurrection. This resulted in Adonijah's execution.

David, however, forewarned his son, "Don't dread these things; don't let them be a source of discouragement. Trust the Lord."

2. Terror. This is a response to an immediate person or situation. When the sailors discovered that Jonah was a Jew fleeing from his God, Scripture says, "This *terrified* them and they asked, 'What have you done?'" (Jonah 1:10, NIV, italics mine). Terror carries with it a sense of helplessness. In the face of an imminent, unavoidable tragedy, we feel terror.

A few years ago I flew from Atlanta to Pittsburgh and the take-off was excessively bumpy. The pilot came on the intercom to announce that he was not sure our landing gear would work and he planned to buzz the Pittsburgh tower so they could do a visual inspection. The pilot said, "If they give us the okay, we'll try to land." Everyone wondered what our options would be. There was absolute silence on our final approach. As it turned out, everything was fine, but the passengers did not know that at the time and their faces showed their terror.

3. Awe. This emotion involves a submissive and admiring fear inspired by authority or power. It is a wondering reverence tinged with trepidation and caused by something lofty and grand.

Early in his kingship, Solomon faced the conundrum of two mothers claiming birthrights to the same child. Trusting in the instincts of the true mother, he suggested cutting the child in half. The one who actually bore the child was immediately willing to give up all claims in order to preserve the baby's life. In this way Solomon discerned who was telling the truth. The Bible says, "And all Israel heard of the judgment which the king had rendered; and they *feared* the king, for they saw that the wisdom of God was in him to administer justice" (1 Kings 3:28, italics mine).

The people of Israel had known leaders who were skillful in battle, capable in command and savvy in diplomacy, but never had they experienced the guidance of a king as wise in the practical ways of life as Solomon. They recognized his wisdom was a special gift from God, and that filled them with a sense of wonder.

If you have met a sports superstar or someone else you hold in high esteem, you know the emotion the Israelites felt. You can hardly believe you have been so fortunate as to meet someone whose skills you admire so much. You experience a sense of awe just being in their presence.

4. Reverence. This involves a feeling of profound respect and devoted deference. It is placing someone or something above the commonplace and responding with utmost loyalty. The Book of Leviticus records many moral and ceremonial laws in the Jewish religion. Among them are the Ten Commandments. The second commandment says, "'Every one of you shall *revere* his mother and his father'" (Lev. 19:3, italics mine). Reverence includes an attitude of respect, but more. It is also a deference— a willingness to bend to the will of another.

When all these facets of fear are put together, we discover that "the fear of the Lord" is not a trembling dread that paralyzes action, but neither is it just polite reverence— a tip of the hat. Many Christians assume that true fear precludes a loving and intimate relationship with God, so they place their emphasis on reverence, and lightly at that. In some worship centers prior to the service, the hubbub frequently sounds more like a flock of hens preparing to lay eggs than a group of people preparing to enter the courts of a holy and righteous King.

In his fictional novel *The Wind in the Willows*, Kenneth Graham portrays two animals in the commanding presence of The Piper. Mr. Graham imagines the following conversation: "'Rat,' the Mole found breath to whisper, shaking, 'Are you afraid?' 'Afraid?' murmured the rat, his eyes shining with unutterable love. 'Afraid, of Him? Oh, never, never. And yet, and yet, O Mole, I am afraid.' And, crouching to the earth, they bowed their heads."[2] That is the kind of fear that the Lord deserves— an eerie awe balanced with an intimacy filled with love.

The attitude

Everything begins with an attitude. Murder, for example, starts with hatred and bitterness. Adultery begins with a casual glance, then the lustful look and finally the act itself.

Worship also begins with an attitude. The "fear of the Lord" found in Proverbs is an attitude falling between the reverential awe for who He is (the God of the universe) and for what He wants (to be intimately involved with our lives in a growing relationship). Upon this fear poises the kind of worship that pleases God.

Keeping in balance

God loves balance. We see it in nature. Meteorologists used to "seed" clouds to prevent hurricanes from forming. Then they discovered that these tropical storms with torrential rains, glaring lightning and rumbling thunder are nature's way of dispersing the oppressive heat that builds up on the equator. Without these balancing agents, one portion of our world would fry and much of the rest would freeze.

God also expects balance in our worship. Humans have an amazing ability to go to excesses. We have either a feast or a famine. But reaching a posture of worship that pleases God is the consequence of mixing a number of attitudes in the right proportions. Fortunately, we have the Bible, God's guide for making the right choices in uniting the elements of balance. This balance is reached by mixing the following attitudes:

Submission to God's wisdom

A friend shared that one of the most traumatic experiences he has encountered as a parent came when his 18-month-old daughter smashed her finger in the garage door. They rushed her to the hospital. In the emergency room the doctors determined that the fingernail had to be removed. Quickly they strapped her to a "papoose board" to keep her immobile and began the surgery using a local anesthetic. All the while she cried, "Daddy! Daddy! Daddy!" and her eyes pleaded for help. It was heartrending, but Daddy knew he had to let the doctors do their work or the finger would be disfigured permanently. Time has proven the wisdom of the decision— her finger is perfectly normal. But the crisis is not forgotten.

Sometimes God allows events that must rend His heart as well. Yet He knows they are necessary for our good. There are possessions, attitudes, even people that need to be cut out of our lives so that we can develop normally— but it hurts both Him and us.

True worship can take place only when we willingly accept what God allows to come into our lives, even though it is painful. No worship is more precious to God than that which comes from a broken but trusting heart. Job exemplified this when, upon receiving the news that his children had all been killed, he "arose and tore his robe and shaved his head, and he fell to the ground and worshiped. And he said: "Naked I came from my mother's womb, and naked shall I return there. The LORD gave, and the LORD has taken away; blessed be the name of the LORD" (Job 1:20–21). Job's worship arose from the raw nerve of life.

The fear of the Lord enables us to welcome God's discipline, suffering, even seeming contradictions in our lives because we stand in awe of His wisdom and know He does only what is best for us. There comes a point when we must let go of our instinct to control, subdue our urge to have the answers for everything and simply let God be God. At that point we are ready to worship.

If we insist on worshiping only what we know and understand, we end up worshiping ourselves. This is evident from a new "politically correct" translation of the Bible published in 1995 by the Oxford University Press. According to one reviewer, it "makes God the 'Father-Mother,' Jesus a 'Child' rather than the Son, and has children 'heed' rather than 'obey' their parents. . . . God's 'right hand' becomes God's 'mighty hand' or his 'side,' so that left-handed people won't feel left out." Elizabeth Achtemeier, adjunct professor of the Bible at Union Theological Seminary in Richmond, Virginia, rightfully observed, "If you want to know the current opinion of so-called scholars, you can read it in this book. . . . In the final analysis, when they change the language, they change God and lapse into self-idolatry. . . . The individual's sensibilities [instead of the Bible] have become supreme."[3]

God's wisdom says, "Every word of God is pure; He is a shield to those who put their trust in Him" (Prov. 30:5). When we submit to Him instead of transitory circumstances or the changing winds of political correctness, we will find ourselves worshiping a God who is big enough to handle all our difficulties.

Intimacy with God's character

The key to intimacy with God is the fear of God. If this seems contradictory it is because in human relationships fear puts up a barrier to intimacy. Not so with God. In his book *Savoring the Wisdom of Proverbs*, Louis Goldberg says, "The proper regard for wisdom and of her reception leads to an encounter with God that not only includes reverential awe but also intimate experience. These two experiences seem to be opposites. How does one stand in awe before a holy God and yet be intimate with Him? How can one fellowship with God and have respect for His holiness? Yet wisdom makes this possible."[4]

In fact, a lack of the awe or reverence we call "fear" indicates we do not know God intimately. Dr. Ed Young wrote, "Reverence is the only appropriate response to God. If we do not revere Him, it is because we have not seen Him as He truly is. It is impossible to behold God in His majesty, mercy, and mystery, and not experience an unbidden holy fear."5 God is so awesome (Deut. 7:21; Neh. 1:5; Jer. 20:11; Dan. 9:4) that whenever He reveals Himself, man's natural response is to fear Him. When Manoah, the father of Samson, saw the Angel of the Lord, he said to his wife, "We shall surely die, because we have seen God!" (Judg. 13:22). Isaiah saw God in the temple and responded, "Woe is me, for I am undone! Because I am a man of unclean lips, and I dwell in the midst of a people of unclean lips; for my eyes have seen the King, the LORD of hosts" (Isa. 6:5).

In this scientific age people trust facts. But some truths cannot be reduced to just the facts— and God is one of them. He bursts the boundaries of our understanding, and we can but fall before Him in uncomprehending yet unquestioning love and loyalty. When we truly experience the presence of God, goose bumps race up and down our spine, the hairs on the back of our neck stand stiff, and our legs turn to rubber. Theologians have a term for this experience; they call it the *numinous*.

This response (the *numinous*) comes from knowing God's character— not just knowing it factually (God is love, God is holy, God is pure) but knowing it experientially. To paraphrase Mark Twain, the difference between *knowing* God's character intimately and knowing *about* God's character is the difference between lightning and the lightning bug.

When the apostle Paul arrived in Athens, he found a very religious people. In fact, they were so religious they even had an altar to the "Unknown God" just so they would not offend a god by leaving him or her out (Acts 17:23). Numerous Christians try to worship a God that is essentially unknown to them. They have no sense of reverence or awe for Him— and that results in an unsatisfying encounter for both God and them. Only as we fear God personally can we worship Him personally.

Hate toward God's enemies

People who have grown up in a Christian environment are thoroughly drilled in the maxim that it is wrong to hate. Yet the Book of Proverbs says, "The fear of the LORD is to hate evil; pride and arrogance and the evil way" (Prov. 8:13). Despite what we may have been taught, there is a place in a balanced Christian life for hate. If we fear God, we will hate what He hates.

This does not mean we shoot abortion doctors and fire-bomb their clinics, but it does call us to respond to the self-ishness and greed that motivate the abortion industry. We do not pray for the spread of AIDS to get rid of homosexuals, but we do confront them with their sin and, at the same time, show them the love of Jesus that can rescue them from it.

Jo Berry observes, "We shrug our shoulders at evil, rela-bel it or ignore it, but we do not detest it. *Hate* is a strong term; it is a consuming emotion. When you hate something, you are repelled by it, hostile toward it and hold it in con-tempt. You loathe and despise it. Those of us who claim we truly worship and adore the Lord will hate evil and find it intolerable, offensive and unbearable."[6]

When it comes to evil, Christians today have forgotten how to hate. In a letter to his constituency, Christian leader James Dobson took to task the evangelical church's response to the United Nations World Conference on Women in Beijing, China. Of the 50,000 delegates and observers from 185 nations, the conservative, Protestant representa-tion was almost nil. As Dobson put it:

> There on the world stage was an event that was unique in the history of mankind. Representatives from 185 nations gathered to discuss issues of vital importance to the human race. Christians had every reason to be alarmed. At stake was the future of the family, the safety of every unborn baby, sexual puri-ty before marriage and the heterosexual basis for marriage. Also under siege was the delicate relation-ship between men and women upon which families

are based. Scripture was mocked and the Christian faith was contradicted. Morality itself was on the line in Beijing— yet the collective voice of the Protestant community was virtually mute. God forgive us![7]

How can we say that we fear God and yet take no stand against evil? The better we know God, the more repulsive sin becomes.

The consequences

When we truly fear God we will worship Him with our whole lives. Worship will not be just a Sunday activity; we will worship all the time.

Brother Lawrence was a cook in a monastery. His life exemplified the opportunities we have to worship. He said,

> I made it my business to be in the Lord's presence just as much throughout the day as I did when I came to my appointed time of prayer. I drove anything from my mind that was capable of interrupting my thought of God. I did this all the time, every hour, every minute, even in the height of my daily business. . . . The time of business does not differ with me from the time of prayer, and in the noise and clatter of my kitchen, while several persons are at the same time calling for different things, I possess God in as great a tranquility as if I were upon my knees at the blessed sacrament.[8]

God never intended for us to segregate our lives into little boxes. We do not worship in one area, entertain in another and work in another. We worship Him with every fiber of our being. Our knowledge and worship of Him are to influence all facets of our lives.

Our intellectual life

Solomon says, "The fear of the LORD is the beginning of knowledge, but fools despise wisdom and instruction" (Prov. 1:7). The word *beginning* means a starting place or a foundation. There is no true education without the fear of the Lord as its starting place. Education that is humanistic is:

- built on the wrong foundation
- headed in the wrong direction
- based on the wrong suppositions
- focused on the wrong things

Without the foundation of the fear of the Lord, knowledge becomes a source of frustration— it only makes us realize how little we know. Life is filled with mysteries. We not only do not know how to cure the common cold, we do not even know how a medication as simple as aspirin works. Man has been driven to many foolish conclusions because he has refused to admit there is One smarter than himself and worthy of his worship.

Prior to his death in 1984, Paul Dirac was called "the world's greatest living physicist." His pioneering discoveries led to the Nobel Prize in physics in 1933 and to the development of quantum mechanics. Called by some the equal of Isaac Newton and Albert Einstein, at age 30 he became the youngest person ever to hold a professorship at Cambridge University.

Once when Dirac was asked why gravitational forces were getting weaker, he responded, "Why? Because God made it so." Dirac insisted that science and religion were not at odds; rather, "they are both seekers after truth." He believed that God used "beautiful mathematics" to create the world. "Beautiful, but not simple. My theories are based on faith that there is reason for all the numbers nature provides us with."

People do not jettison their intelligence when they become Christians. God even says, "Come now, and let us *reason* together" (Isa. 1:18, italics mine). There is a necessary place for the intellect in the Christian life. Yet when we fear God, we know that there are some things about Him and His creation that we will never understand. This should motivate us to worship Him. But there's more.

Our physical life

Proverbs 10:27 says, "The fear of the Lord prolongs days, but the years of the wicked will be shortened." Our nation has sown a godless public life, and now we are reaping a crop of violence and death. Instead of being killed in wars, our young men are being killed on the streets.

Consider the case of Joseph Morales. Morales was slain September 24, 1995—three days after his 21st birthday—while standing with a group of other young men on a street corner in San Francisco. Several young men walked up. One or two of them pulled out guns and opened fire, killing Morales and wounding a 17-year-old boy nearby. To add to the tragedy, Morales was the third generation in his family to meet a violent death. His mother was killed in April 1978 and his grandmother in April 1971.

Unfortunately, the violent death of Joseph Morales is not unique. One of his relatives rattled off the names of four other young men who had been killed in that same area within the last two years. He observed, "It used to be easier to keep them on track or at least get them on a good path if they got in trouble. But these days these young men just kill each other too fast."[9]

God's Word is not a lucky rabbit's foot or some magical enchantment to keep us safe; but when we follow His wisdom, we avoid many situations and places where we can be harmed. Solomon says, "The fear of the LORD is a fountain of life, to avoid the snares of death" (Prov. 14:27).

Our emotional life

People were asked in a survey, "What is the basic feeling you have about life?" Sixty percent answered, "Fear." People are afraid of uncertain economic times, deteriorating health and the spiritual darkness of our world. They are afraid for their families, their jobs and their futures.

Such fears have a legitimate basis. Companies such as IBM, AT&T and General Motors historically have provided jobs for thousands, but now they are laying off large numbers of their work force. On the health scene, viruses and bacteria are mutating and are no longer responsive to treatments that once were effective in destroying them. Despite the fall of communism in Europe, the future is still clouded by civil wars raging in countries that once were stable because of an iron fist. Men and women are quickly abandoning what little hope they had. God's wisdom, however, says, "In the fear of the LORD there is strong confidence, and His children will have a place of refuge" (Prov. 14:26). God's Word gives us an assurance of the future.

Billy Graham was conducting an evangelistic crusade in London and had the privilege of meeting Winston Churchill. Mr. Churchill asked him, "Is there any hope for this world?" Dr. Graham replied, "Yes! I have read the last chapter of the Bible and it says we win." We need not fear the future. God's wisdom gives us the confidence to face a deteriorating world with hope and courage.

In fact, those who have learned to fear God discover they have nothing else to fear. Charles Spurgeon said, "He who comes forth fresh from beholding the face of God will never fear the face of man." As they buried the Scottish reformer John Knox, it was said, "Here lies one who feared God so much that he never feared the face of any man."

Some people think that the opposite of fear is courage. But a person can be fearful and courageous at the same time. During World War II, a military governor met with General George Patton in Sicily. When he praised Patton highly for his courage and bravery, the general replied, "Sir, I am not a brave man— the truth is, I am an utter craven coward. I have never been within the sound of gunshot or in sight of battle in my whole life that I wasn't so scared that I had sweat in the palms of my hands." Years later, when

Patton's autobiography was published, it contained this significant statement by the general: "I learned very early in my life never to take counsel of my fears."

No, the opposite of fear is not courage— it is contentment. That is why Solomon could write, "Better is a little with the fear of the Lord, than great treasure with trouble" (Prov. 15:16). Great treasures are often accompanied by great fears— the fear of having the treasure stolen, the fear of being liked only because of your treasure, the fear of investing your treasure foolishly, the fear that you or your family will be harmed because you have a treasure. Such fears destroy our contentment.

When we experience the awe and reverence of God's character, however, even a little becomes a lot. Dr. C. H. Morrison tells the story of a friend who used to collect for charities in a Scottish village. One of the cottages she had to visit was that of a pious and revered old woman named Betty, who, though poor, would have been insulted if the collector had passed the door. One day when the woman called, Betty was sitting at tea. She rose to get her widow's mite out of the chest and threw her apron hastily over the tea table. In curiosity the friend peeped under and saw the hidden cup was filled with water. "Why, Betty," she cried in astonishment, "it isn't tea you've got here; it's water!" "Aye, my dear, it's just water," Betty replied. "But He makes it taste like tea!"

The fear of the Lord is not only good for the mind and body, it's good for the heart as well.

Come, let us worship

The hymn writer invites us, "O worship the King, all glorious above, and gratefully sing His pow'r and His love; Our shield and Defender, the Ancient of days, pavilioned in splendor and girded with praise."

When we know the fear of the Lord, how can we do anything else!

[1] A. W. Tozer, *Whatever Happened to Worship?* (Camp Hill, Pa.: Christian Publications, 1985), p. 9.

[2] Kenneth Graham, *The Wind in the Willows* (New York: Charles Scribner & Sons, 1960), p. 127.

[3] James D. Davis, "'PC' Bible draws praise, condemnation," *Indianapolis Star*, September 24, 1995.

[4] Louis Goldberg, *Savoring the Wisdom of Proverbs* (Chicago: Moody Press, 1990), p. 43.

[5] Ed Young, "Reverence," *Moody*, September 1995, p. 16.

[6] Jo Berry, *Proverbs for Easier Living* (Ventura, Calif.: Regal Books, 1980), p. 30.

[7] James Dobson, *Focus on the Family Newsletter*, October 1995, p. 5.

[8] Frank Laubach and Brother Lawrence, *Practicing His Presence* (Goleta, Calif.: Christian Books, 1973), pp. 64, 105.

[9] Jim Zamora, "Mother and grandmother of Joseph Morales were also killed," *Electronic San Francisco Examiner*, November 16, 1995, via the Internet.

Chapter 4

Wisdom and Your Happiness

Happy is the man who finds wisdom.
Proverbs 3:13

Everybody wants to be happy, but most people look for happiness in all the wrong places. Some search for an elusive happiness in promiscuous living; others in their work or their family. But happiness is the fruit of God's wisdom, and if you are to find it, you must search for happiness in the right place and pursue it in godly wisdom.

As Benjamin Franklin was concluding a stirring speech on the guarantees of the U. S. Constitution, a heckler shouted, "Aw, them words don't mean nothin' at all. Where's all the happiness you say it guarantees us?" Franklin smiled and replied, "My friend, the constitution only guarantees the American people the right to pursue happiness; you have to catch it yourself."

Much of our happiness depends on our attitudes toward it. Is wanting to be happy a sin? Should you settle for the misery of a misunderstood life, or does God want you to enjoy your earthly life? Is happiness the most important thing to you? How you view happiness will largely determine your answers to these questions. What is your attitude?

An inconsistent attitude

There are two extremes in the pursuit of happiness. One is represented by the American playwright George Bernard Shaw, who said, "I don't want to be happy because I don't have time for such a luxury." A surprising number of Christians fall into that camp. They feel that happiness is somehow akin to sinfulness. A little girl visited a farm and was impressed with an old, rawboned workhorse she found in the barn. Looking into his doleful eyes, she exclaimed, "Oh, horsey, you must be such a good Christian— your face is so long!"

This approach, however, is inconsistent with nature. Why would God make smiling so healthy for us (it produces fewer wrinkles than frowning) if He did not want us to engage in it? It's also easier. It takes 72 muscles to frown and only 14 to smile. In addition, researchers have found that people who are not satisfied with their life increase their risk of premature death by at least ten percent. Unhappiness, it appears, is not compatible with good health (Prov. 17:22).

This attitude also does not fit Christ's lifestyle. Jesus must have had a sense of humor, a characteristic associated with happy people. How else can we explain such comical illustrations as a man with a plank in his eye (Matt. 7:3-5) or a camel trying to crawl through the eye of a needle (Matt. 19:24)? Isaiah called Him "a Man of sorrows and acquainted with grief" (Isa. 53:3), but Jesus was not doleful every moment. He enjoyed good times with friends. He attended parties like the wedding feast at Cana in Galilee, and He evidently entered into the spirit of the occasion (John 2:1-11). He was even falsely accused of being a glutton and winebibber by the stuffy Pharisees (Luke 7:34). This certainly does not sound like a man who avoided happiness as though it were a sin.

An inappropriate attitude

The other extreme goes much farther back in time. It predates the Greek philosopher Aristotle (384-322 B.C.), but he expressed it best when he said, "Happiness is the meaning and the purpose of life, the whole aim and end of human existence." A lot of people today would agree. They consider happiness the chief aim of life. Life is a perpetual party and they never take anything seriously, especially their responsibilities. These are the people who move out of an apartment in the middle of the night and stiff the landlord with several months' back rent. They frequent the party scene but refuse to drive responsibly on the way home, often driving with impaired senses due to alcohol consumption. They care little for their family, their parents or their friends. They are self-centered and hedonistic.

For a Christian, happiness is not the "aim and end of human existence." To adopt this philosophy is to place yourself and your pleasure at the center of your world. That does not mean Christians are unhappy people; who has more to be happy about than one whose sins are forgiven and who is certain of heaven? But Christians do not tune their lives, their fortunes and their futures to the rhythm of happiness.

Unfortunately, the pursuit of happiness is one of the most common pursuits in our society today. Perhaps the little boy who asked, "Mom, when can we go to Toys-R-Mine?" epitomizes the attitude toward happiness for most people. Selfishness and self-centeredness may get us what we want, but they will not make us happy.

A biblical attitude

From a biblical perspective, happiness is a by-product of right choices, and right choices are the result of godly wisdom. Happiness comes to us when we are confident that God is perfect and just. Life is unfair, and we will be unhappy if we think it should be. But life's fairness is not the issue; God's fairness is the issue of happiness. If we believe that God is sovereignly controlling the events of our lives so that what happens to us is ultimately for our good and for His glory (Rom. 8:28), we will find a measure of happiness even in the tough times of our lives. Happiness is a peace of mind that confronts the storms of life with the steadfastness and stability of a deeply rooted tree. None of this happens by chance. The key is to make our choices based on God's Word.

Happiness is neither to be avoided as though it were wrong or sought for as the primary good in your life. The Bible teaches that happiness can be yours if you look for it in the right places and in the right way. "He who heeds the word wisely will find good, and whoever trusts in the Lord, happy is he" (Prov. 16:20).

Looking for happiness

In his book *Hope for the Troubled Heart*, Billy Graham observed, "Americans have more wealth, more two-car families, more private homes and write more books on how to be happy than any other country."[1] A Louis Harris Poll revealed that 97 percent of Americans rank happiness as their number one concern. But a close observation of most American lifestyles indicates that they have not found it and don't know where to look. Let's barricade some blind alleys in the pursuit of happiness.

It cannot be found in simplicity

Epicurus (341-270 B.C.) was the founder of the school of Epicureanism, a philosophy that says intellectual pleasures are superior to sensual pleasures (although this became corrupted in later centuries to mean the exact opposite). He said, "If you want to make a man happy, add not to his riches but take away from his desires."

A modern and growing movement in our world, especially in America, strongly agrees. Garden books and magazines urge people to compost their organic waste products instead of sending them to the landfill. Municipalities are organizing recycling programs for glass, plastic, aluminum and paper. Car manufacturers are poised to offer vehicles that burn cleaner alternative fuels. We often hear the slogan, "Live simply that others may simply live."

This is good! There is much truth in Epicurus' philosophy. Dr. Karl Menninger once asked a wealthy patient,

"What on earth are you going to do with all that money?" The patient replied, "Just worry about it, I suppose." Dr. Menninger went on, "Well, do you get that much pleasure out of worrying about it?" "No," the patient responded, "but I get such terror when I think of giving some of it to somebody." What freedom and joy some people could experience if they simply deleted some of their desires rather than added to their riches.

Yet simplistic living— a return to the basics— is not the complete answer. Go into the inner cities or into some rural areas of the United States, and you will find people living very simply (in poverty), but they aren't happy. Most of us could do with a great deal less than what we have and it would be good for us, but it would not necessarily make us happy.

It cannot be found in secularism

Karl Marx made the famous statement, "Religion is the opiate of the people." He also said, "The first requisite for people's happiness is the abolition of religion." Yet Marx himself was extremely unhappy. His biographers, even those who were sympathetic to communism, described him as "isolated and bitterly hostile," "irritable," "insensitive" and "jealously suspicious."

Others have tried to deny God in order to find happiness but without success. The French philosopher Francois Marie Arouet (better known under his assumed name, Voltaire) refused to believe that one could have a personal relationship with God. He penned numerous articles against religion, especially Christianity. Yet when he was near death, he wrote, "I wish I had never been born." Obviously, he did not discover the secret to happiness. No one can factor God out of his life and expect to find happiness.

It cannot be found in stoicism

Stoicism, another product of Greek philosophy, emphasized the necessity of rising above one's passions and desires. Good and evil were to be greeted with the same tranquility and steadfastness. Stoicism is still alive and well. It is reflected in the British "stiff upper lip" and in the American expression, "You gotta do what you gotta do!"

King George V expressed it this way: "The secret of happiness is not to do what you like but to like what you do." Again, this has some validity. Too often we feel sorry for ourselves and indulge in a pity party when what we really should do is get on with what we need to do. As Abraham Lincoln said, "Most folks are as happy as they make up their minds to be."

Nevertheless, some tasks may simply exceed our ability to "like what we do." We may do it because we have to, but to try to convince ourselves that we like it is utter foolishness. I go to the dentist to have my teeth drilled, filled, polished or pulled, but I don't like it. Being stoic about unhappy happenings is certainly not the secret to happiness.

It cannot be found in pleasure

An almost universal delusion is that happiness is found in people and things that give us pleasure. This may be true in the short term, but such happiness is momentary. The English writer and poet Lord Byron gave himself to all sorts of pleasures. In his later years, however, he wrote, "The worm, the canker, and the grief are mine alone."

Merle Haggard, winner of the Academy of Country and Western Music's top male vocalist many times, sings that the good times are here today, let's not think about tomorrow. Still, tomorrow does come, doesn't it? And often it brings with it deadly consequences from the "happiness" we enjoyed today. Anyone who has overdosed on drugs can tell you the truth about momentary happiness.

If pleasure is the well from which springs our happiness, what will we do when the well runs dry? Pleasure comes from athletic ability, money, youth and sex. But what becomes of our pleasure when such a quality of life no longer exists? People become old. They become poor. Their happiness becomes only a faint memory. There must be more to happiness than this.

It cannot be found in wealth

Not all of us have the opportunity to test the theory that wealth brings happiness. Most of us wish we did. But you do not have to be wealthy to learn that happiness does not always accompany wealth. Just ask those who have been wealthy and unhappy.

Bill Curry of south Boston worked most of his life as a cafeteria cook for the Merit Food Company. His income was modest, but he managed to provide for his wife and their son and daughter. So when Bill won a $3.6 million state lottery, his first thought was just to buy a Dalmatian puppy for the children. That was the extent of his celebration. But then the parasites converged— the lawyers and investment advisers, the accountants and financial analysts. Bill was so overwhelmed by them and by people wanting handouts for charities that he died of a heart attack at age 37. It's evident that wealth did not bring him the happiness most people thought it would.

Multimillionaire Andrew Carnegie once said, "Millionaires who laugh are rare." No, you do not have to be rich to discover that riches do not bring true happiness. Wealth is just another blind alley to the pursuit of happiness.

God's happiness

All the evidence points to the fact that the secret to happiness is not found in simplicity, secularism, stoicism, pleasure or wealth. These are the places where the world encourages us to look, but ultimately we find they are only shallow pools and not the springs of happiness that we were promised. We will never find happiness in them because it just isn't there.

If we cannot find lasting happiness in these things, we might be tempted to think it cannot be found at all. But the Bible says differently. You can find happiness if you know were to look. Proverbs 3:13 tells us where. Solomon, who had wealth, pleasure and everything else, boldly said, "Blessed is the man who finds wisdom, the man who gains understanding." Happiness is found in God's wisdom.

The word *blessed* (Hebrew: *esher*) comes from the verb meaning "to go straight or to make progress, to set right." It can be translated as "happy." Knowing this, we can conclude that happiness is a by-product of going straight, being on the right path, making real progress toward God and Christian maturity. It is the consequence of having a right relationship with God the Father through Jesus Christ, His Son. Happiness is not the result of raucous living; it is the reward for righteous living.

A life lived skillfully, a life that filters every decision and experience through the pages of God's Word, is certain to be a happy life. Proverbs wisdom, not worldly wisdom, guides us through the pitfalls and traps that could rob us of lasting happiness.

If we pursue the happiness that comes only through God's wisdom, we should expect to see some tangible results from our discovery of divine wisdom. We are not disappointed. Here are some of the consequences that Proverbs promises from the pursuit of happiness through heaven's wisdom.

Long life

Solomon maintains, "Length of days is in her right hand" (3:16). Even secular thought is recognizing that physical health and spiritual health are related. For example, a recent medical research reported new evidence linking heart disease and anger. According to an Associated Press release, Dr. Redford B. Williams Jr. and some of his colleagues conducted a personality study on 118 students in law school. The students were graded on their hostility. Twenty-five years later, 20 percent of those who had scored highest as being angry persons had died, compared with only 5 percent of those who had registered lowest. Anger not only hurts your spiritual life, it shortens your physical life (Prov. 22:24–25).

Other studies also indicate that religion is not only good for the soul but good for the body. A research team led by medical sociologist Kenneth F. Ferraro of Purdue University found that people who regularly worship say they feel healthier than those who don't. Of those who said they do not worship regularly, 9 percent reported poor health and 26 percent claimed excellent health. Among the regular worshipers, just 4 percent said they were in poor health, while 36 percent reported excellent health (Prov. 3:7–8; 14:30; 17:22). This same study found that the Sabbath rest is another plus for healthier living. Setting aside a day for a change of pace and some relaxation appears to have beneficial results.[2]

God's wisdom is beneficial to both heart and soul. The happiness of a long life finds its origin in His wisdom.

Riches and honor

Often, riches and honor do not go together. The lifestyles of the wealthy and the well-known seldom stand for purity and righteousness. Often the consequences are tragic. In April 1995, Cheyenne Brando, daughter of film star Marlon Brando, committed suicide after her live-in boyfriend was murdered by her half-brother, Christian Brando. In June 1995, Hugh Grant, an up-and-coming young movie star, was arrested by members of the Los Angeles vice squad for lewd conduct with a prostitute in public. In August 1995, Jerry Garcia, lead guitarist for the rock group the Grateful Dead, died of an apparent heart attack after years of hard living and drug abuse.

Only when we allow God's wisdom to guide our lives can riches and honor coexist. But coexist they can! The Bible offers examples of people like Job, Abraham and Joseph of Arimathea who were men of wealth as well as men of honor.

When combined with godliness, wealth can be used as an instrument to facilitate our happiness and the happiness of others. The choice is not between God's wisdom and wealth; the choice is between God's wisdom and folly. It takes the wisdom of God to keep a proper perspective on wealth.

Pleasant paths

Years ago, when a king planned to visit an area of his kingdom, men were sent ahead to cut a road and remove any obstacles that might make the trip unpleasant. In the same way, God's wisdom smoothes our paths. Solomon says, "Her ways are ways of pleasantness" (3:17).

The wisdom of God, the kind of wisdom we find in the Bible, smoothes out the bumps on life's road. If you want your life to be rocky and turbulent, live the life advised by worldly wisdom. But if you want your life to journey gently over high plains, live the life advised by godly wisdom. Does this mean your life will always be as smooth as a newly paved highway? Not in the least. But Proverbs wisdom will help you steer clear of the potholes of sin and folly. For example, godly wisdom tells you not to sin when you are angry (Eph. 4:26). It reveals the secret of forgiveness (Matt. 6:14–15). It levels the bumps of bitterness (Eph. 4:31) and flattens out the anxieties of care (1 Pet. 5:7).

God's wisdom warns of pitfalls and obstacles and offers routes to avoid them. The man who chooses to ignore this wisdom is bound for an unpleasant trip and an unhappy life.

Peace

Solomon continues, "And all her paths are peace" (Prov. 3:17). Peace is a scarce commodity these days. But unless there is peace in our hearts there can never be peace in the world. Only through wisdom can we come to know the God of peace and the peace of God. To know the God of peace means we have a personal relationship with Him through His Son, Jesus Christ (1 John 5:12–13). This is not an intellectual relationship; it is a surrender of all that we are to all that He is. When that happens, His Holy Spirit brings into our hearts a peace that "surpasses understanding" (Phil. 4:7).

When we are in turmoil, when we are filled with fear and apprehension, we cannot be happy. Only a total trust in the One who created us and the One who saved us can replace these "joy stealers" with "peace givers."

A pilot was experiencing difficulty in landing his plane because of fog. The airport decided to bring him in by radar. As he waited to receive directions from the ground, he suddenly remembered a tall pole in the flight path. In a panic he reminded the control tower about it. The reply came bluntly, "You obey instruction. We'll take care of the obstructions."

Wisdom reminds us that happiness comes as we trust God to take care of the problems. There will be challenges in your life, but nothing He cannot handle. It is His paths, not yours, that lead to a happy and peaceful destination.

Evaluating the outcome

Wisdom is essential to happiness. Lasting happiness can no more exist apart from wisdom than a fish can live apart from water. Little wonder Solomon said, "For her proceeds are better than the profits of silver, and her gain than fine gold. She is more precious than rubies, and all the things you may desire cannot compare with her" (Prov. 3:14-15). *Profits* and *gain* are the terms of a trader or investor. The happiness that wisdom returns to us is of greater value than anything that gold or gems can buy. If you want the best return on your investment, invest in godly wisdom and you will enjoy happiness as a return.

We are like the little boy who went to the pet shop to pick out a puppy. His father pointed out all the choices and asked, "Which do you want?" The youngster was fascinated by one of the puppies whose tail wagged ferociously. The little guy quickly answered, "I want the one with the happy ending." In the end, we all want happiness. How blessed is the man or woman who has learned that living by the wisdom of God brings a happy ending. Everything else falls far short.

---

[1] Billy Graham, *Hope for the Troubled Heart* (Dallas: Word Publishing, 1991), p. 10.

[2] Anita Manning, *USA Today*, October 19, 1992, p. 1D.

Chapter 5

Wisdom and Your Wealth

Honor the LORD with your possesions.
Proverbs 3:9

A book entitled *The Day America Told the Truth* reported a survey that asked adults what they would be willing to do for $10 million. Twenty-five percent of the respondents said they would abandon their entire family. Twenty-three percent said they would become prostitutes for a week for that kind of money. About 16 percent said they would be willing to leave their spouse, and 3 percent would even put their children up for adoption.

Obviously, Americans value money very highly. When the American Council on Education surveyed 200,000 incoming freshmen in 1987, 71 percent said they were going to college so they could get a high-paying job. Now that these same individuals are in the work force, they have charged more than half a trillion dollars of goods and services on some 350 million major credit cards.

Money is also a prominent topic in Scripture. John MacArthur, well-known pastor and author, notes that 16 out of 38 of Christ's parables deal with money; more is said in the New Testament about money than heaven and hell combined; and five times more is said about money than prayer. MacArthur asserts that while there are 500-plus verses on both prayer and faith, there are more than 2,000 verses dealing with money and possessions.

God is concerned about money and possessions because they are vital to our lives. We trade a certain portion of our lives in terms of hours and days for an agreed-upon amount of money. When you purchase an $800 couch, you could say you are trading 80 hours of your life (if you are paid $10 an hour) for that piece of furniture.

Since we have a limited number of days here on earth, God is legitimately concerned about how and what we trade the hours of our lives for. Time is a precious, non-renewable resource. We have neither time nor money to waste.

God knows equally well that how we spend the hours of our lives today will influence how we spend eternity. Christians have a special obligation to use time (represented in part by money) in a way that will store up for us riches in heaven.

In addition, when we receive Christ as our Savior, not only do we become His in body and soul, but all we have is His as well. As Martin Luther astutely observed, "There are three conversions necessary for a believer: the conversion of the heart, mind and the purse." Of these three, it may be that Christians in our society find the conversion of the purse the most difficult. Our purse belongs to God (all of it, not just ten percent), and He is rightly concerned about how we use His finances.

Principles of stewardship

These truths underscore the importance of following God's wisdom in making and using wealth. Many sources offer advice on finances, but none are as valuable as the Bible. Perhaps we can best understand God's wisdom by examining five major principles from the Book of Proverbs that every Christian should know, faithfully practice and pass on to his children.

1. Wealth is the product of work

Work is an honorable enterprise. When God put Adam and Eve into the Garden of Eden, even before the Fall, He gave them work to do. Genesis 2:15 records, "Then the LORD God took the man and put him in the garden of Eden to tend and keep it." Work became more difficult after man's rebellion. God said, "Cursed is the ground for your sake; in toil you shall eat of it all the days of your life" (Gen. 3:17). But work itself is not a curse.

Despite the complications caused by Adam's and Eve's sin, work always has been God's way for man to gain wealth. As the latter part of Proverbs 13:11 reminds us, "He who gathers by labor will increase."

Unfortunately, a growing number of people are convinced there has to be an easier way. As a consequence, they spend their energy and often their hard-earned cash on schemes to get rich quickly. Among other things, this makes them vulnerable to:

Unscrupulous scams

People eager to take your money have been around for a long time (remember Jacob and his uncle, Laban?). Scam artists have found that the same tricks work in every generation, primarily because people who are eager to get rich quickly are already primed to take the bait. They snap up that "hot" real estate deal offering them a surefire opportunity to triple their investment in just a few years. Then there's the once-in-a-lifetime stock investment opportunity. Who can resist that? What about those certified, risk-free oil well ventures or the purchase of silver or platinum? Over the centuries, we still have not learned that there are no free lunches.

What motivates this behavior? Greed, the desire to strike it rich. But the wisdom of Proverbs says, "A faithful man will abound with blessings, but he who hastens to be rich will not go unpunished" (Prov. 28:20). Hard work and investing what we earn are God's methods of accumulating wealth, not the world's fast-buck schemes.

Addictive gambling

Perhaps the biggest scheme for losers is gambling, the fastest growing industry in the United States. At present, 38 states and the District of Columbia have state-sponsored lotteries. Lottery players spent $30 billion in 1994, compared with $9 billion in 1985. Eleven percent of the 1,416 people surveyed by *Money* magazine said the best way to get rich is to play the lottery.[1] This is alarming when we realize that gambling is just as addictive as drugs or alcohol. In fact, some claim that the newer forms of gambling (such as electronic machines in stores and bars or interactive TV betting at home) are more addictive than cards and roulette wheels were in past decades.[2]

Gambling devastates the family. Those who can least afford it— the poor and the working class— tend to spend the greatest portion of their income on gambling. Once the gambler is hooked, his family quickly loses importance. For example, in Beatrice, Nebraska, a young father left his three-year-old child and his nine-month-old baby in the car while he went indoors to play keno. The children had been inside the vehicle for about half an hour before police were called to rescue them.[3]

Addicted gamblers reason, *The next roll of the dice, the next pull of the arm, the next lottery ticket will be the lucky one, and all my problems will be over.* But it does not work out that way, and God knows it. We cannot circumvent His plan for accumulating wealth anymore than we can circumvent His plan for salvation.

Stealing

When we think of stealing, we usually conjure up someone shoplifting or robbing banks. These actions certainly fit the definition. Instead of working to earn the money to purchase an item, the thief chooses the easy way— simply steal it. It's fast, easy and, unless he is caught, quite profitable.

But there are other ways to steal. Selling a used car to a stranger and claiming it is in mint condition (when it needs a new engine and a set of shocks) is a form of stealing. Taking a coffee break longer than allowed is stealing. Writing a check when you know there are no funds to cover it is a form of stealing.

Stealing may provide us with the things we want—and more quickly than if we were to work for them—but God forbids it. The eighth commandment clearly say, "You shall not steal" (Ex. 20:15). So stringent were God's laws against stealing that Exodus 22:1 notes, "If a man steals an ox or a sheep, and slaughters it or sells it, he shall restore five oxen for an ox and four sheep for a sheep." Imagine how we could reduce burglaries and thefts today if the thief were required to return what he had stolen plus a 20 or 25 percent penalty payment.

The bottom line, however, is that thievery harms not only the one who is stolen from but the one who steals as well. Proverbs 21:7 says, "The robbery of the wicked shall destroy them" (KJV). When we try to get rich quickly by resorting to dishonesty, the end can only be tragic.

2. Money is God's gift to us for ministry

The world's view of money is reflected in the attitude of a young woman from Boise, Idaho, who in June 1995 won an $87.6 million Powerball jackpot. When asked what she would do with all that money, she replied, "If I want it, I'll buy it." Her thinking had become clouded by her inability to know God's purpose for allowing us to have money.

Money is power. Money is influence. But God sees money as an opportunity for investment in the lives of others. Proverbs 22:9 says, "He who has a bountiful eye will be blessed, for he gives of his bread to the poor." In Proverbs 28:27 we are told, "He who gives to the poor will not lack, but he who hides his eyes will have many curses." The purpose of having is giving, as demonstrated in the following ways:

Invest in the local church

God would have us invest in our local church. This is where most Christians get much of their spiritual nourishment, and as Scripture says, "You shall not muzzle an ox while it treads out the grain" (Deut. 25:4). Without the ministry of the local church, other ministries would have a difficult time existing. The local church provides workers for the harvest, accountability for missionaries on the field and financial support for many other ministries. To neglect it is to sever the lifeline to the wider work of Christ.

A Christian woman once said to a friend, "Our church costs too much. They are always asking for money." Her friend replied, "Years ago a little boy was born in our home. He cost me a lot of money too. He had a big appetite. He needed clothes, medicine, toys and even a puppy. Then he went to school, and that cost a lot more. Later he went away to college and that cost a small fortune! But in his senior year at college he died, and since the funeral he has not cost me a penny. Do you think I would rather have the money or my son?"

It costs money to operate a vibrant church, but the alternative— to try to get along without the local church— is unacceptable. If you belong to a Bible-teaching church, support it faithfully. It deserves your support.

Invest in ministry

Our opportunities and responsibilities for supporting the work of the Lord, however, do not end with our local assembly. They extend to every area of our lives where Christ is blessing us.

A man once visited a Quaker meeting. He was unaware that Quakers are known for their "Quiet Meetings," called such because everyone sits quietly until the Spirit moves someone to speak. As time passed the man began to get impatient. Finally he leaned over and whispered to his neighbor, "When does the service start?" His neighbor replied, "Sir, the service begins just after this meeting ends." Ministry is not just what happens for a few hours on Sunday and maybe on Wednesday night. When we go forth from our meetings and our services, we go to serve— and that can be expensive.

Investing our finances, talents and time for the service of Christ around the world is the responsibility of every Christian. Our Commander-in-chief invested His all in saving men and women; so should we. Many years ago there was a great missionary rally held in the Royal Albert Hall in London, England. The Duke of Wellington, who had defeated the armies of Napoleon Bonaparte, was there. A clergy turned to him and asked, "My Lord Duke, do you believe in missions?" The Duke replied with the question, "What are your marching orders?" The man responded, "Well, the Bible says we're to go unto all the world." "Then," said the Duke, "you have nothing to say about it. As a soldier, you simply obey orders."

Whether God calls you to invest by going or giving, you must hold nothing back. The spiritual reward you will receive in return far exceeds the temporary concerns about committing all you are and all you have to the ministry of the Word.

Invest in your future

Have you seen the bumper sticker that says, "Get even. Live long enough to be a problem to your children"? This is easier to do than it once was: life expectancy for Americans 200 years ago was 35 years; today it is 79. But it is not God's desire for us to be either a burden or a problem to our children. One way to avoid this is to invest in our future.

The tragic fact is that most people approach retirement age with grossly inadequate funds. The Social Security Administration found that 75 percent of retirees depend on friends, relatives or Social Security as their only source of support, and as many as 25 percent of persons older than 65 must continue to work out of financial necessity. LIAMA Cooperative Research claims that 93 percent of men who are age 65 and who have failed financially say it was because of a lack of a definite plan.

One of the wisest pieces of advice given to me when I was young was, "Live like Christ is returning at any moment; plan as though it will be a thousand years." The wisdom from the Book of Proverbs says, "Go to the ant, you sluggard! Consider her ways and be wise, which, having no captain, overseer or ruler, provides her supplies in the summer, and gathers her food in the harvest" (6:6–8). God will take care of us, but wise stewardship is part of His plan for our future.

Invest in your family

Family life has become incredibly confused in the last decade or more. An example of this confusion was reported in *Newsweek* magazine. Bill Wyman, of the rock group Rolling Stones, married a woman 34 years younger than he. Bill's son, Stephen, married a woman who was 16 years his senior. That's strange, but stranger still is that Stephen's wife is the mother of Bill's wife.[4] Imagine the confusion created by the marriage of Bill's son to Bill's mother-in-law! Today, families are desperately trying to resolve confusing relationships, but many fail because they refuse to follow God's wisdom.

God sees the family as the most important earthly investment you can make. In a profile article in *USA Today*, Billy Graham says that if he were starting out again, he would "travel less, speak less and study more and spend more time with my family."[5]

You cannot buy love but you can buy time, and most families spell love T-I-M-E. Dads, invest in your daughters by taking them out to breakfast and spending some loving time with them. It may be the most important breakfast meeting you schedule all week. Hire a baby-sitter and go out with your wife. Don't just tell her you love her; show her you love her as well. Use occasions like these to encourage and edify those who mean so much to you. Proverbs 17:6 says, "Children's children are the crown of old men, and the glory of children is their father." Invest liberally in your family. They are your most important personal investment.

3. Money is God's gift to us to honor Him

Someone once said, "Show me what a man does with his money, and I'll show you what's important to him." Jesus said, "For where your treasure is, there your heart will be also" (John 6:21). Notice that it is the heart that follows our treasure, not the other way around. Our investments rule our heart. Money is as much a test as it is a tool. It reveals our priorities.

When the Bureau of Economic Analysis (a division of the U.S. Department of Commerce) researched what Americans spend their money on, they found that, among other things, Americans spent:

$4.1 trillion on food and tobacco

$600 billion on housing

$463.1 billion on transportation (buying cars, upkeep, etc.)

$318.8 billion on recreation

$282.4 billion on clothing, accessories, jewelry

$116.2 billion on charitable giving (both Christian and non-Christian).[6]

The most bloated budgets reflected items of personal gratification. We Americans spend almost three times as much on recreation as we do on charity (this is before we deduct gifts to non-Christian groups such as the United Way, the American Heart Association, etc.). We spend more than twice the amount on clothing and accessories as we do on global evangelism. If our hearts are where our treasures are, for many people it would seem that their heart has never left home.

God is honored when we give Him first place in our finances. Our gifts to Him need to come off the top of our paycheck, not out of the leftovers. God blesses those who are faithful in first-fruit giving. Do you know what the following people have in common: J. C. Kraft of Kraft Cheese Corporation, Henry Crowell of Quaker Oats, William Colgate of Colgate Soap, Wallace Johnson, founder of Holiday Inns, and J. C. Penney of J. C. Penney stores? They all put God first in their lives and businesses. They began their businesses by asking God for wisdom in running them according to Christian principles. They expressed their dependency on Him by giving a tithe of their income and soon graduated to giving God's work more than 25 percent of their profits.

These business entrepreneurs were not content to give God leftovers, and God was not content to bless them with leftovers. They were not content to be casual in their stewardship but tested God according to His promise in Proverbs 3:9-10: "Honor the LORD with your possessions, and with the firstfruits of all your increase; so your barns will be filled with plenty, and your vats will overflow with new wine."

God's wisdom says, "There is one who scatters, yet increases more; and there is one who withholds more than is right, but it leads to poverty. The generous soul will be made rich, and he who waters will also be watered himself" (Prov. 11:24-25). Use your income to honor God, and He will use His wisdom to honor you.

4. Money is not God's solution for every problem

A trap that many people fall into, including Christians, is thinking, *If only we had a little more money, our problems would be solved.* Studies have shown that most people think about 20 percent more income would satisfy them. These same studies, however, indicate this is true across all financial levels. The person making $100,000 a year is as likely to want just 20 percent more as a person making $20,000 a year. Lack of money gets blamed for many things, but it is seldom responsible.

Money cannot provide marital harmony

According to a report from Brown University, financial problems are a major cause of divorce in 80 percent of couples under 30 years of age. While this may be true, being wealthy is no deterrent to divorce. Just look at some Hollywood stars. A few years back *Forbes* magazine listed the top 40 income-producing entertainers.[7] Number two on the list was Michael Jackson (now separated from Lisa Marie Presley) at $100 million; Steven Spielberg was fourth at $87 million (two marriages); Sylvester Stallone was seventh with $63 million (two marriages, five and a half years in a "relationship" and currently engaged); and Johnny Carson was eleventh with $50 million (four marriages).

If money could buy marital harmony, these people should have been wed blissfully for a long time. It is obvious that neither the abundance nor the lack of money is the decisive factor in making marriages work; the real secret is being content with what you have.

Money cannot provide security

Security is a big issue these days. Drive-by shootings on our city streets, muggings in broad daylight, murders in the midst of busy restaurants— all these and more have left people understandably jittery. A survey taken in a major metropolitan area found that 53 percent of the more than 13,000 people who returned the questionnaire said they did not feel safe on that city's streets. Twenty-seven percent of the respondents said they did not feel safe from crime while at home.[8] Owen Hanson rightly observed, "Western civilization has advanced to where we bolt our doors and windows at night while jungle natives sleep in open huts."

How have people reacted to the curse of crime on our streets and in our homes? They have purchased extra locks for their doors, installed elaborate security systems and bought guard dogs. Those with sufficient resources have even hired personal bodyguards. Obviously, these people hope they can buy their safety. God knew all about this. In

Proverbs 18:11 He said, "The rich man's wealth is his strong city, and like a high wall in his own esteem."

Such a hope, however, is fruitless. Political assassinations are common despite armed soldiers present for protection. Well-known personalities have been killed despite their wealth: John Lennon, of the Beatles, was gunned down on a public street; Selena, a young and rising music star, was killed by the woman who had been hired to manage her boutiques; Maurizio Gucci, grandson of the founder of Gucci, was shot to death in the foyer of a downtown Milan building. Money can give the illusion of security but not the reality.

Money cannot save from wrath

In a depressed mood, author Thomas Carlyle once said, "God sits in heaven and does nothing." It may seem that way sometimes, but don't be deceived. God is busily moving all of human history toward a "Day of Wrath" (see Job 21:30; Prov. 11:4; Zeph. 1:15; Rom. 2:5). Such a day is required because God is just. He cannot allow His laws to be broken and His righteousness flaunted without responding in judgment. Besides, how could a loving God not be filled with wrath towards those things that hurt and destroy us, His prized creation? Don't be fooled; wrath will come!

But don't misunderstand God's wrath. God is not just a peeved deity— a kind of cosmic, ill-tempered Mr. Zap who indulges in violent displays of anger when we do not do what we ought. Wrath is God's way of saying to man, "Look, you must face the truth. I created you for Myself. If you decide that you don't want Me, then you will suffer the consequences." God will not withhold His wrath because His moral integrity insists that disobedience be punished and obedience be rewarded.

The day of God's wrath is not to be taken lightly. Ted Turner, multimillionaire TV mogul, told folks at a Baptist church luncheon, "I'm looking forward to dying and going to hell because that's where I'm headed." If he knew anything about his destination, he would not be so eager to go there.

Jonathan Edwards described hell as "that world of misery, that lake of burning brimstone, extended abroad under you. There is the dreadful pit of the glowing flames of the wrath of God; there is hell's wide gaping mouth open; and you have nothing to stand upon, nor anything to take hold of."[9]

It is foolish to take God's wrath lightly! It is equally foolhardy to think that money can keep us from His wrath. Proverbs 11:4 says, "Riches do not profit in the day of wrath, but righteousness delivers from death." Hell is an eternal separation from God (which the Bible calls "death," as in Revelation 20:6). The only way to be delivered from such death is through righteousness, or a right relationship with God the Father through His Son, Jesus Christ. Wealth cannot buy that relationship. It comes only when we trust Jesus as our Savior. Only Jesus can save us from the wrath to come (1 Thess. 1:10).

5. Only eternity is ultimately important

It looked as though both the hero and the heroine of the Western movie were doomed. They were surrounded by a pack of cattle thieves intent on making sure neither left that place alive. One of the little boys in the front row of the theater sniffed, "If he had kept his eye on the gang instead of the girl, this never would have happened!"

Unfortunately, all of us are guilty of having our eyes on the wrong thing— especially when it comes to the matter of eternity. We get so caught up in the here and now that we forget eternity is far more important.

Eternity will last an awfully long time (in fact, using *eternity* and *time* in the same sentence is an oxymoron; they don't logically belong together, like *sanitary* and *landfill*). God's wisdom urges us to face the fact that the earthly part of life is brief (Prov. 27:1) and that we will spend far more of our life in eternity than anywhere else. Therefore, we need to look at our accomplishments as we will see them on eternity's morning, when our earthly years will be behind us. What will be important on that great and glorious morning?

Money? No, that will be gone, never to come back again. Position? That will have passed away forever as well. Pleasure and comfort? Those, too, will be irrelevant.

But we will value two things with all our being: the first is to know that God had His way and His will in our lives, and the second is to know that precious souls whom we influenced are standing around God's throne.

We make an eternal investment when growing in the grace and knowledge of our Lord Jesus Christ is a priority in our lives. We have an eye on eternity when we give of our substance and of our time to help others come to know Christ as their Savior. Jesus commanded us to "lay up for [our]selves treasures in heaven, where neither moth nor rust destroys and where thieves do not break in and steal" (Matt. 6:20). All other monetary investments pale by comparison.

True wealth

Money is so empty and unsatisfying that we are amazed at what people will do to get it. Murder, sexual immorality, deception and much more have been motivated by the desire for money.

In the end, most people find wealth vain. Sir Ernest Cassel, a friend of kings and emperors, a multimillionaire who spent vast fortunes for the benefit of mankind, said to one of his visitors, "You may have all the money in the world, and yet be a lonely, sorrowing old man."

There is, however, a wealth that does satisfy. God's wisdom says, "Riches and honor are with me, enduring riches and righteousness" (Prov. 8:18). This wealth may not fatten bank accounts or open doors to a rich and famous lifestyle, but it lasts far beyond this lifetime. When we live a life consistent with God's wisdom, we have at the minimum the riches of love, peace, joy and all the other spiritual fruit, which money cannot buy.

Even more important, such a life is one without grief.

Proverbs 10:22 says, "The blessing of the LORD makes one rich, and He adds no sorrow with it." We cannot escape the sorrows of a sin-filled world, but we can avoid the misery of a sin-filled life. The riches of God's wisdom guide us through the pitfalls and snares that make many other lives a sorrowful experience.

Material wealth is not bad— it's simply inadequate. God wants to make you rich, so don't settle just for money!

[1] Associated Press, "Survey finds Americans worry less about wallets," *Lincoln Star*, April 12, 1995, p. 3.

[2] Editor, "Gambling: Laying morals aside," *Lincoln Journal Star*, March 5, 1995, p. 4C.

[3] Associated Press, "Beatrice man cited for leaving children in keno parking lot," *Lincoln Star*, April 1995, p. 8.

[4] *Newsweek*, April 12, 1993, p. 66.

[5] *USA Today*, May 1, 1992, p. D-5.

[6] *The World Almanac and Book of Facts 1994*, CD-ROM.

[7] The income was the combined gross income for the years 1989 and 1990.

[8] Associated Press, "Omaha residents don't feel safe on city streets, survey reveals," *Lincoln Star*, February 26, 1995, p. 2.

[9] Jonathan Edwards, Sermon: "Sinners in the Hands of an Angry God."

Chapter 6

Wisdom and Your Spouse

*Houses and riches are an inheritance from fathers,
but a prudent wife is from the LORD.
Proverbs 19:14*

No subject has given rise to more humor than marriage. A marriage counselor asked a couple, "When did you first start having disagreements?" The wife responded, "It all began when he wanted to be in the wedding photos."

Then there's the wife who was crying because the dog ate some food she had prepared for her husband. Attempting to console her, the man said, "Don't worry, honey. We'll buy another dog."

Despite the humor, however, marriage is no laughing matter. It is one of life's most challenging relationships. As someone noted, "Marriage is like eating with chopsticks. It looks easy until you try it." Yet it also has the potential for being life's most satisfying relationship. William Lyon Phelps wrote, "The highest happiness on earth is in marriage. Every man who is happily married is a successful man even if he has failed in everything else."[1]

Given the complex nature of marriage, we should look for help in developing this relationship only from the best of sources. A computer dating service is not the answer. Marriage involves more than being "compatible" on a computerized questionnaire. Many people have found that even friends who try to fix them up with someone cannot be trusted completely.

God's Word is the only dependable source for guidance in this important life choice. After all, marriage was God's idea. Genesis records, "So Adam gave names to all cattle, to the birds of the air, and to every beast of the field. But for Adam there was not found a helper comparable to him. And the LORD God caused a deep sleep to fall on Adam, and he slept; and He took one of his ribs, and closed up the flesh in its place. Then the rib which the LORD God had taken from man He made into a woman, and He brought her to the man" (Gen. 2:20-22). Out of Adam's lack came Eve's life.

God's wisdom offers the kind of advice we need both before we get married and afterwards. Obviously, the best time to look to God for direction is before you tie the knot. Therefore, let's consider some biblical wisdom.

Before you say "I do"

The premarital period is a time to learn about each other and about yourself. It is a time to investigate your mutual likes and dislikes, your goals and your spiritual attitudes. Serious thought should be given to the following questions:

Why am I getting married?

Proverbs 18:22 says that "he who finds a wife [or a husband] finds a good thing." But good things can be spoiled by bad motives. Someone has said that marriage doesn't create problems; it reveals them. That will certainly be true if you enter marriage for the wrong reasons.

Abusive homes. Some people want to marry in order to escape a troubled home life. Wanting to leave home because of physical and/or sexual abuse is understandable. If you have suffered such abuse, however, seek help from your pastor or other professional who can guide you into biblical forgiveness and restoration. The person you marry may not be equipped and should not be expected to deal with this unresolved pain in your life. It could deal a damaging blow to your marriage.

Unhappy homes. Others who want to marry in order to leave home are more likely to be dealing with personality conflicts. Perhaps you think your dad and mom are too strict and have too many rules. Maybe you feel they don't understand you or even care about you. It could be that they simply get on your nerves and you want to get married just to get away from them.

Running from these problems into marriage is only preparing yourself to run into additional problems. Stay and work through them before you marry. In the process you learn how to strengthen a troubled relationship, and that will be invaluable training for working out problems in your marriage. If you run now, you will likely run again when there is trouble in paradise.

Loneliness. Other people want to get married because they are lonely. All their friends are married and seem happy. They want to share their life with somebody too. The pain of loneliness is genuine. Of course, companionship is a legitimate goal for marriage, but it is a poor basis for one. Some people marry for companionship and find marriage more lonely than being single. If your spouse has a job that takes him or her away for long periods at a time, if he or she works late each night, you sometimes live in solitary confinement. God's wisdom says, "Better to dwell in the wilderness [i.e., alone, with nothing or no one around you], than with a contentious and angry woman" (Prov. 21:19). That's true for angry men too.

Marriage provides opportunity for physical intimacy, but loneliness can be cured only by emotional intimacy. One of the most common reasons wives seek counseling is that they are "lonely in their marriage." Most people assume if two people share the same house and the same bed they cannot possibly be lonely. But this is a cruel and hollow myth, as too many married people can attest.

Emotional intimacy requires a willingness to be vulnerable, use of good communication skills and a strong desire to cherish each other. Marriage provides opportunity for the latter, but only time and effort can bring about the other two.

Uncertainty. A few people decide to marry because they don't know what else to do with their lives. They are finished with high school or college and are at loose ends. The prospect of living the single life is so frightening they latch onto the first available person and hope for endless happiness.

The fallacy of this approach should be obvious: the only One who can give us a real happiness is God. The moment we try to make a man or woman the focal point of our universe we set ourselves up for disappointment. Humans are fallible—they make mistakes. Unhappiness results. They are finite, so they get sick and die. Again, unhappiness comes. They are weak, so they cannot always meet our needs. Unhappiness follows. Only God is big enough to rise to the challenge of providing endless happiness. Marriage is not the answer when we are lonely, trapped in an abusive household or uncertain about what to do with our lives. There is much more to making the marriage commitment than that.

If these are all the wrong reasons for getting married, what are the right reasons? There is primarily one—marriage is for the glory of God.

As two people consider making this life-changing alteration, they need to ask themselves, "Will God be more glorified through us as a couple than through either of us as individuals? Can we do more to further God's kingdom by establishing a godly home and perhaps raising a family than we can by serving Him as single people?" Rarely are such questions asked before marriage.

If the Lord intends for you to marry (and He does select a few individuals to remain single), and if you are planning to marry for the right reason, then by all means follow God's plan for your life. Yet you still need to ask yourself another question.

Who is a qualified partner?

It may seem obvious that you should seek a qualified person to marry, but many people today are confused about what makes a qualified candidate for a good marriage relationship. Let's explore some issues related to this question.

Opposite sex. Until the last few decades I didn't think I would have to deal with this issue in writing about marriage, but today nothing can be assumed. Therefore, let me state that the first qualification for a potential spouse is that he or she be of the opposite sex. Same-sex unions, men marrying men or women marrying women, are not God's will for marriage. While such unions are sanctioned by some churches, they are never sanctioned by God. Scripture makes it clear that homosexuality and lesbianism are sins that God finds particularly disgusting (Lev. 18:22). While the Almighty offers hope to the homosexual (1 Cor. 6:8-11), He offers no blessing on their sin.

Salvation. Your spouse must be a believer. Solomon says in Ecclesiastes 4:12, "Though one may be overpowered by another, two can withstand him. And a threefold cord is not quickly broken." That threefold cord in a marriage is the groom, the bride and Jesus Christ. The New Testament echoes this same thought in 2 Corinthians 6:14–15, where Paul counsels, "Do not be unequally yoked together with unbelievers. For what fellowship has righteousness with lawlessness? And what communion has light with darkness? And what accord has Christ with Belial? Or what part has a believer with an unbeliever?"

Paul is not promoting an "I'm-better-than-you-are" attitude in these verses. He is simply warning that if one spouse is not a believer, the couple will lack common purposes and goals. One person in such a marriage is headed for heaven and the other for hell. One is seeking to serve Christ; the other serves only himself. One is led by the Holy Spirit, while the other is governed by his lusts and passions. One is seeking to further God's kingdom; the other is hindering it. A believer and unbeliever may appear on the surface to be in harmony, but there is no spiritual or eternal common ground in their marriage.

Before seriously dating someone, you are well advised to talk about spiritual matters with him or her. Almost never does a believer win an unbeliever to the Lord after marriage. Don't get burned as so many others have. Follow God's guidelines in dating, and you will follow them in marriage.

Godly character. The one we marry ought also to have a godly character. Wisdom says, "Better to dwell in a corner of a housetop, than in a house shared with a contentious woman" (Prov. 21:9). Don't think a penchant for contentiousness or quarreling is limited to women. Proverbs 26:21 says, "As charcoal is to burning coals, and wood to fire, so is a contentious man to kindle strife." A nagging wife or overbearing husband is difficult to live with. Just ask their spouse.

Before you marry, watch how your potential mate responds to his or her parents and siblings. A person's character is revealed in the way he treats those who are close to him. Proverbs 19:26 says, "He who mistreats his father and chases away his mother is a son who causes shame and brings reproach."

Godly character, on the other hand, expresses itself in a servant mentality. A spouse with godly character views his part in the marriage as an opportunity to give, not just receive. He or she looks for ways to build up the partner, especially in his or her walk with the Lord. Godly spouses find fulfillment in striving to achieve the roles for husbands and wives set forth in Scripture. That is the kind of person you want to marry. It may not be someone like dear old dad, but it is someone like your Heavenly Father.

Look before you leap

Next to receiving Christ as your Savior, choosing the person you will spend the rest of your life with is the most important decision you will ever make. So don't be in a hurry to come to a conclusion. That is why your dating period should be long enough to know whether or not you want to pursue this person seriously as a spouse. Dawson Trotman, founder of the Navigators, used to say, "There are quick decisions and good decisions. There are no good quick decisions." Be patient— God is not in a hurry. You shouldn't be either.

One way to get into shape physically is through isotonic exercising. Push against an immovable object like a post or a wall. You won't budge it, but the wall's resistance strengthens your muscles. God sometimes makes us wait, not to deny us anything but to build our spiritual muscles so we can make the right choices.

Make your decision to marry a matter of much prayer. Flipping a coin, pulling petals off a daisy or any other legendary method of decision making will not do your marriage justice. You wouldn't make other, less important decisions that way. God wants you to use wisdom whether you are buying a car, selecting a place to live, choosing a college to attend or looking for the right person to marry.

Don't be afraid to end a relationship that does not meet God's standards. It could save you a world of heartache. A broken relationship does not mean you will never marry. If God plans for you to marry, trust Him to bring the right person along for you. Remember, the only thing worse than not having a spouse is having the wrong spouse.

Courtship is the time to learn all you can about this one who might be your future mate. Take it seriously. Take it slowly. Take it spiritually. Once the vows are said and the commitment is made before God and other witnesses, God's Word says it's too late to change your mind.

But God's wisdom does not end when you walk down the aisle. It also applies to your married life.

After you say "I do"

A cartoon in *Bottom Line/Business* magazine shows a man and a woman sitting in a living room. She says to him, "Look, I'm not talking about a lifetime commitment. I'm talking about marriage."[2]

Tragically, this reflects the attitude of many people toward marriage. Someone has suggested we would be better off if, instead of marrying for better or worse, people would marry for good. There are six truths we need to recognize if we want to make our marriage last:

1. Recognize the divine involvement in your marriage

Those who study and write about the marriage relationship frequently talk about the power of hormones, the importance of social factors, the impact of financial matters, etc., on an individual seeking to get married. Undoubtedly, these do influence the choice and compatibility of marriage partners. What these experts fail to recognize, however, is the divine component in marriage that sometimes overrides all of this. Wisdom says, "He who finds a wife . . . obtains favor from the LORD" (Prov. 18:22).

Changing your partner

Whether or not God has just one "perfect" mate per person, it is still His influence that ultimately brings a marriageable couple together. As in other areas, we must yield to the mystery of God's sovereignty and man's free will. Both are at work.

Take great care, then, before you decide to change what God has given you. I read with amusement the story of the bride who was highly nervous before her wedding day. The pastor suggested she concentrate on just three things. "First, as you start to come toward the front," he told her, "concentrate on the aisle. About halfway down, lift your head and look at the altar. When you get down to the altar, your groom will be waiting for you, and all you have to do is concentrate on him. If you remember to do those three things, you will have no problems."

The next afternoon, when the organ began to play, the young bride started down the aisle, her forehead creased in grim concentration. The guests who were within earshot were astonished to hear her saying over and over to herself: "Aisle altar him. Aisle altar him. Aisle altar him."

Amusing, yes, but also dangerous. God has a purpose for every trait your spouse possesses. We are to edify and encourage one another— even challenge one another to grow in our walk with the Lord. But are we to set about changing our mates, molding them in our preconceived image? No, the changing is best left up to the Lord. We can inform, but only God can transform.

Therefore, when a Christian enters into marriage, the word *divorce* should exit from his vocabulary. We need to put aside any thought that we may have married the wrong person. From the moment you take your vows before God, that person becomes the right person. He or she is the individual God will use to shape and mold your character. God makes a commitment to this relationship. He will not suggest, "Maybe you should find someone else," and neither should you!

If you have violated one or more of God's principles in selecting a mate (see pages 82-84), the road may be bumpier and the trip less pleasant. That, however, doesn't alter anything. Relationships are not always designed just for your comfort. Sometimes they are designed just for your good.

A matter of trust

Marriage really comes down to a matter of trust. Will you trust God to use the person you have married to knock off your rough edges, smooth out your wrinkles and cause you to draw closer to Him? You might say, "But I really messed up. He isn't a Christian." Search your Bible and you will find that God used non-Christians numerous times to get His will done (Pharaoh, Nebuchadnezzar and Caesar, to name just a few). God is able to work with imperfect situations just as He works with imperfect people. This is not an excuse to violate His principles, but it is a reason to not despair.

Every marriage has a touch of the divine. You may have a wonderful relationship or you may have a difficult one, but God has a purpose for it.

2. Recognize the friendship factor in your marriage

Despite the emphasis on the physical aspect of love that we see in movies and on television, most couples are really looking for a good friend. When your spouse is not only your lover but your best friend, the chances for a "till-death-do-you-part" marriage are greatly enhanced.

In a survey involving 100,000 couples, researchers concluded that passionate love lasts an average of two years. If the husband and wife are not good friends at the end of this time, their marriage will likely die.[3] Women often say that what they really want is their husbands to tell them, "You're the best wife a man could hope for. You're my best friend." Friendship will see a marriage through more troubled water than sex will.

Friendship between husband and wife must be preserved the way any other friendship is perpetuated. God's wisdom makes it clear that:

We need to avoid gossip. Whenever we share a fault or a failure with someone who is not part of the problem or the solution, we are gossiping. Many married people expose their spouse's shortcomings to others more for the sake of hurting than helping. They may make a humorous remark at a family get-together, but underneath the humor is the desire to let others know what an inadequate person the husband or wife is. This is nothing more than gossip!

Have you ever watched an icicle melt? It doesn't disappear all at once. Instead, it melts one drip at a time. No one drip makes that much difference, but together they consume the whole.

Gossiping about our spouse can do the same thing. A little cut here and a little jab there, and eventually the marriage dies. There are appropriate people to talk to when we have concerns: pastors, marriage counselors or health care professionals (not friends or relatives; they are rarely good options). Furthermore, this should be done privately and in the strictest confidence. The damage that gossip does to a marriage is sometimes impossible to repair. Wisdom says, "He who covers a transgression seeks love, but he who repeats a matter separates friends" (Prov. 17:9).

We need to treat our spouse courteously. Isn't it strange that we often favor strangers with more respect than we do our spouse? When we are with a group of people we don't know well, we say, "Please" and "Thank you." We hold the doors open in public buildings for those we have never seen before and probably will never see again. These are appropriate acts of courtesy, but they need to be extended to our spouse as well. When was the last time you opened the car door for your wife? When was the last time you sincerely thanked your husband for something he did around the house? Proverbs 15:23 says, "A word spoken in due season, how good it is!"

Courtesy should start at home and overflow to other places. Concentrate on showing an attitude of respect and thoughtfulness to the person whom God intends to be your best friend, and it will come automatically in other situations. "A word fitly spoken is like apples of gold in settings of silver" (Prov. 25:11)

We need to work at it. Few things come naturally, and a profound friendship is no exception. Friendship can tolerate everything but neglect. It takes effort to cultivate the emotional intimacy necessary for something more than a shallow relationship. We need to spend time learning to communicate on a feeling level rather than "just the facts." Evaluate the types of conversation you have with your spouse. Are they mostly about how the kids are doing, what bills need to be paid and whether it will be hot or cold tomorrow? If topics like these form the bulk of your conversation, you need to consider a change. Schedule a time for your spouse and you to be alone together. Make up a list of topics ahead of time that will draw your spouse into a deeper conversation. Formulate questions that cannot be answered factually but will reveal feelings and opinions. Wisdom says, "Counsel in the heart of man is like deep water, but a man of understanding will draw it out" (Prov. 20:5).

Friendship should never be the sole basis for marriage, but a marriage without friendship is as incomplete as a rose without a fragrance. If you commit yourself to being a friend as well as a spouse, your friendship will grow deeper and deeper. Men, think of your spouse in this way:

> God gave to me a precious friend
> As precious as my life;
> But I choose not to call her friend,
> I choose to call her wife.

3. Recognize the shared responsibilities in your marriage

The comic strip *Cathy* showed her down at the office with all her friends going crazy over her new engagement ring. Cathy is racked with doubt, torment and anguished. But no one is paying any attention to her feelings. Finally, in exasperation, she exclaims, "Everyone wants a piece of the rock but no one wants a chunk of the puddle."

That describes many marriages. The partners like the privileges that matrimony provides, but they don't want the obligations. Nevertheless, for a marriage to last, God's wisdom says that spouses need to share responsibilities.

Both husband and wife are responsible for child training. Proverbs 1:8-9 says, "My son, hear the instruction of your *father*, and do not forsake the law of your *mother*; for they will be a graceful ornament on your head, and chains about your neck" (italics mine). Both parents are important to a child. For example, a study once disclosed that if both mom and dad attend church regularly, 72 percent of their children remain faithful. If only dad attends, 55 percent remain faithful; if only mom, then 15 percent. If neither parent attends regularly, only 6 percent of their children will remain faithful to the church.[4] The statistics speak for themselves— it takes both parents to have the maximum influence.

As the table below indicates,[5] parents (especially fathers) in the United States need to rethink their idea that raising children is the "wife's responsibility."

Which parent spent the most time with the children when they were young?

Area of responsibility:	Mother Alone	Father Alone	Both Equally
Caring for health needs	71%	7%	22%
Discussing religion	48	11	35
Talking about life	48	12	38
Disciplining	43	22	34
Playing games	42	17	40
Teaching values	40	8	52

A one-parent family is definitely not an ideal in God's wisdom. Raising a family requires that both parents share the responsibility. An absentee father or mother (or sometimes, both) won't do the job.

4. Recognize the need for ardor as well as faithfulness

Every marriage must begin with faithfulness. Without the trust and stability created by steadfast loyalty, the probability of a long-lasting relationship is slim. But faithfulness is a dying commodity in our fast-paced world.

The nature of our times is reflected in a letter sent to columnist Abigail Van Buren. A man wrote, "Dear Abby: I am in love and I am having an affair with two different women. I can't marry them both. Please tell me what to do, but don't give me any of that morality stuff." Abby's answer is a zinger. "Dear Sir: The only difference between humans and animals is morality. Please write to a veterinarian."

God's wisdom says that even the wounds of a faithful person are more desirable than the flattery of one who lacks faithfulness (Prov. 27:6). A marriage cannot be blessed unless both parties are committed to loyalty.

But we cannot stop at faithfulness. As good and necessary as that is, ardor is important to a successful marriage as well. Proverbs 5:19 instructs the husband, "As a loving deer and a graceful doe, let her breasts satisfy you at all times; and always be enraptured with her love."

The word *enraptured* in this verse literally means "to reel or to be intoxicated." It is most frequently used of the excesses of sin, but not here. Instead, it is an encouragement for husbands and wives to freely give themselves to each other. In plain terms, Solomon says, "Let there be passion—but let it be limited to your wife or husband."

This is especially significant considering the condition of our society. The immorality of today is much like it was in the city of Corinth during the apostle Paul's time. In that situation he urged, "Nevertheless, because of sexual immorality, let each man have his own wife, and let each woman have her own husband. Let the husband render to his wife the affection due her, and likewise also the wife to her husband" (1 Cor. 7:2-3). The physical aspect of a relationship is important, but it must be fully satisfied within the boundaries of marriage.

Passion is designed by God and is not wrong if it is directed toward the right object. The seductress purrs, "I have spread my bed with tapestry, colored coverings of Egyptian linen. I have perfumed my bed with myrrh, aloes, and cinnamon. Come, let us take our fill of love until morning; let us delight ourselves with love" (Prov. 7:16–18). But this should be the wife's line, not the adulteress's.

Passion apart from marriage never brings the happiness it promises. Proverbs 5:20 asks a penetrating question, "For why should you, my son, be enraptured by an immoral woman, and be embraced in the arms of a seductress?" Why, indeed, would we want to passionately give ourselves to someone who is not committed to us? It's madness. It's sin.

5. Recognize the consequences of an unloved spouse

God's wisdom says, "For three things the earth is perturbed, yes, for four it cannot bear up: for a servant when he reigns, a fool when he is filled with food, a *hateful woman* when she is married, and a maidservant who succeeds her mistress" (Prov. 30:21-23, italics mine). The word translated as "hateful" is the Hebrew word *sane* (pronounced "saw-nay"). Some translations render it as "odious" or "hateful," but it also can be turned around to mean "hated" or "unloved." In the context of Proverbs, this latter translation makes good sense.

A woman who is unloved can become hateful. The bitterness and disappointment of her marriage may sour her whole personality. The next time you meet someone people call a "shrew," consider the fact that she might be an unloved lover.

Men tend to be better at passion than love. They can be consumed by momentary arousal but fail in carrying out the routine, day-in and day-out responsibility of caring for the woman God gave to them. Perhaps that's why the apostle Paul specifies husbands when he says, "Husbands, love your wives, just as Christ also loved the church and gave Himself for it" (Eph. 5:25). Again in Colossians 3:19, Paul says, "Husbands, love your wives and do not be bitter toward them."

When either spouse wanes in his or her love for the other, it becomes painfully evident without words ever being spoken. One husband told of a moment when his youngest son asked, "What do people say when they get married, Dad?" He answered rather uncertainly, "Oh, they promise to love and be kind to each other." After some thought, the youngster innocently said, "You're not always married, are you, Dad?" We cannot hide how we feel!

On the other hand, loving your spouse can result in some unexpected benefits. After analyzing a body of recent demographic research, Linda Waite, the president of Population Association of America, reports that the implied lifetime commitment that comes with marriage reduces stress, improves health and increases wealth. Married couples are financially better off because they are more likely to pool and invest their money. Married men, moreover, tend to make more money than their single pals— 4.5 percent more among blacks and 6.3 percent among whites. More money, Waite argues, means less stress and better medical care.[6]

Naturally, this does not mean a perpetual state of honeymoon bliss. Many challenges can suck a marriage dry: overcommitment to work, illness, financial difficulties. The appropriate response, however, is not to get a divorce and find someone else to love. Instead, you need to renew your love relationship with your spouse. As someone has said, "A successful marriage requires falling in love many times, but always with the same person."

6. Recognize the potential viability in your marriage

Even marriages that were not made in heaven can be made to last. It is always too soon to give up and throw in the towel. Married couples who claim they have never had an argument in 40 years either have poor memories or a dull life. The secret is to refuse to capitulate to the enemy, Satan. The destruction of marriages and families are high on this archfiend's priority list.

Furthermore, our society has played right into the devil's hands by offering divorce as a panacea to every problem. When the Gallup Organization polled teenagers of divorced parents, 71 percent said they did not feel that their parents tried hard enough. A study of divorced couples with preschool children shows that after a year of divorce, 60 percent of men and 73 percent of women feel they made a mistake and should have tried harder to make their marriage work.

Instead of responding to family feuds by making a divorce more difficult to obtain, the world makes it even easier. In Tampa, Florida, you can now get a divorce without leaving your car. Drive-thru divorces! Magazines catering to those who are newly divorced or thinking about divorce cover such subjects as legal considerations, dating hints and advice for reentering the job market. In fact, they cover every subject but one— reconciliation.

We need to remember that in any marital difficulty, both sides bring their own set of problems. With men, it is the proverbial ego. With women, it is basic insecurities that result in contentious talk (nagging).

God actually gave us these particular traits to bless our marriage. Used properly, they can draw a husband and wife together. A woman's insecurities can cause her to turn to her husband for safety and support. And what can be more ego-massaging for a husband than to provide for the needs of his wife?

Sin, however, has twisted and perverted these gender traits until they have become lethal weapons in Satan's hands. Husbands have allowed their egos to become so overblown that they need more stroking than the average wife can offer (or should). Consequently, they look to things outside of their marriage— work, sports, other women— to meet their ego needs.

Wives, on the other hand, have chosen to meet their need for security by nagging. If their husbands don't respond to a request because it doesn't meet their ego needs, wives will try to nag them into doing what they ought. The result is annoying. God's wisdom says, "A continual dripping on a very rainy day and a contentious woman are alike" (Prov. 27:15).

Into the midst of this tangled web steps Jesus Christ. One of Horace's rules of dramatic art was that a god would never be introduced into the action unless the plot had gotten itself into such a tangle that only a god could unravel it. Many marriages today certainly qualify for divine intervention. In Christ there is hope for even the most messed-up marriage.

When the husband turns to Christ, God will help the man deal with his pride and ego. When the wife turns to Him, she will find that Christ will meet her deepest need for security. Even if her husband fails her, God never will.

With Christ as the glue that binds a couple together, even a broken marriage can be restored and possess a strength it never had before. The solution is divine, not divorce.

Couple bonding

From before you say "I do" and all through the years after you say "I do," one of the goals of God's wisdom is to bond a husband and wife together. Why? To form a stable environment in which children can be raised in the fear and admonition of the Lord and His grace and mercy can be shown to the world around us.

The world is hungry to see marriages that work. They know that their approach is bankrupt, but they have no viable option with which to replace it. It is up to Christians to show that through the wisdom of God's Word and the power of God's Spirit, we can offer an alternative.

Why not spend some time today or this weekend bonding with your spouse? Socrates once asked, "Is there anyone with whom you talk less than your wife?" You can change that if you want. Couple bonding is simply taking God at His Word and following the wisdom provided in the Book of Proverbs, God's guide for life's choices.

---

[1] Lillian Eichler Watson, editor, *Light From Many Lamps* (New York: Simon and Schuster, 1951), p. 248.

[2] *Bottom Line/Business*, October 1, 1995, p. 12.

[3] Lowell Lundstrom, *Heaven's Answer for the Home* (Springdale, Pa.: Whitaker House, 1985), p. 21.

[4] Warren Mueller, *Homemade*, May 1990.

[5] Barna Research Group, Ltd., *Family in America* survey, February 1992. This data reflect the answers of 519 parents with children under the age of 18.

[6] *U.S. News & World Report*, April 24, 1995.

Chapter 7

Wisdom and
Your Children

*Now therefore, listen to me, my children,
for blessed are those who keep my ways.*
Proverbs 8:32

Children are our most important treasure. Scripture says, "Happy is the man who has his quiver full of them; they shall not be ashamed, but shall speak with their enemies in the gate" (Ps. 127:5).

They are also our greatest challenge. Providing for them, protecting them from the wrong influences and bringing them up in the nurture and admonition of the Lord is a full-time occupation for parents. The tragedy is that many parents don't take this task seriously. They allow the lure of materialism or fame to draw them from their responsibilities.

Socrates wrote, "Could I climb the highest place in Athens, I would lift my voice and proclaim: 'Fellow citizens, why do you turn and scrape every stone to gather wealth, and take so little care of your children, to whom one day you must relinquish it all?'" Many people have learned to invest in their careers, but they have failed to invest in their children.

God's wisdom says, "Train up a child in the way he should go, and when he is old he will not depart from it" (Prov. 22:6). The word translated here as "train" is used elsewhere to mean "to dedicate," as in a house (Deut. 20:5). Successful parenting takes extraordinary dedication and wisdom. Fortunately, God's Word has some guidelines.

Lessons to teach

We are all teachers. We teach our children almost every waking moment of the day. The question is, what are we teaching them? They are learning from what they hear and see in our lives. They are learning from what we trust and what we question. They are learning from what we say they ought to do but don't do ourselves. God's wisdom gives guidelines for what we must teach our children, but we also must follow those guidelines as parents in how we conduct our own lives. If we fail in our conduct, the lessons we teach will be destroyed by the lessons we model.

Teach your children to attain wisdom

Wisdom doesn't mean you know all the answers; it means you know where to look for the answers. Many people look to sources outside the Bible for their standards. As one self-proclaimed agnostic said, "We make our own Bibles, but they are secular. We turn to science, literature, poetry and history to find what best speaks to us."[1] Others look to personal experiences.

People who reject the Bible in favor of the teachings of men are foolish. God says, "The fool has said in his heart, 'There is no God'" (Ps. 14:1). Those looking for guidance from their own personal experiences (even "religious" experiences) are opening the door to deception because Satan can appear as an angel of light (2 Cor. 11:14). Parents need to instill in their children the truth that there is only one sure guide for life's choices— God's Word.

Proverbs 1:2 says that we are "to know wisdom and instruction." Thus, we need to teach our children the Word of God. It will provide a solid foundation of wisdom and instruction for all of their lives.

In 1874, while the Scriptures were under severe attack by critics, John W. Haley published a defense entitled *Alleged Discrepancies of the Bible*. In the preface he wrote, "Finally, let it be remembered that the Bible is neither dependent upon nor affected by the success or failure of my book. Whatever may become of the latter, whatever may be the verdict passed upon it by an intelligent public, the Bible will stand. In the ages yet to be, when its present assailants and defenders are moldering in the dust, and when our very names are forgotten, [God's Word] will be, as it has been during the centuries past, the guide and solace of millions." How true!

Teach your children to exercise discernment

Furthermore, parents need to teach their children how to discern between worldly wisdom and godly wisdom. Proverbs 1:2 also says that we are "to perceive the words of understanding." That is, our children should be taught to think things through to an intelligent conclusion and not automatically accept as truth everything the world tells them. This is especially important as the world becomes more and more out of step with God's Word.

The world says, "Take control and be in charge."

Our Father says, "I know the plans I have for you— follow Me."

The world says, "Love things and use people. That's the way to get ahead!"

Our Father says, "Love people and use things. That's the way to live!"

The world says, "Keep on the go. The busier you are, the better."

Our Father says, "Come unto Me and I will give you rest."

The world says, "Sacrifice to reach the top. Nothing else is as important."

Our Father says, "The least shall be great— so humble yourself and serve."

The world says, "Everything is relative—it's up to you to decide."

Our Father says, "Thou shalt . . ."

The world sees the outside—the glitz and the glamor.

Our Father sees the inside—from Him you cannot hide.

As you watch television with your children or read stories to them, ask, "Who is speaking here? Is it our Heavenly Father, or are these the words and ideas of men?" Even as you pass billboards advertising products or services, ask the same questions. Make it a family game, but one with a significant purpose. Our children need to know when the world is speaking and when the Lord is speaking. Then they must decide whom they will listen to.

Teach your children what is right

Many young people no longer know what is right and wrong. Moral absolutes have been rejected, so we are left with no moorings for our standards.

In questioning 5,000 young people in grades 4 through 12, Harvard University psychiatrist Robert Coles and other researchers found that children in the United States are becoming morally illiterate, reflecting to some degree the morality of the society in which they live. The researchers found that some children (16 percent) look to God or Scripture to determine what is right. Twenty-five percent base their decisions on what would be best for everyone involved, and another 20 percent on what is generally accepted in the community. Eighteen percent do what makes them happy, 10 percent do whatever they think will improve their situations, and another 11 percent have no form of logic or reasoning at all to help them. Questioned about a specific moral situation, 21 percent of elementary students and 65 percent of high school students said they would be willing to cheat on a major exam.

Proverbs 1:3 says we are to teach our children "to receive the instruction of wisdom, justice, judgment, and equity." That is, we are to teach them to know what is right or wrong. We cannot rely on educational institutions or the community to do our job for us.

Scripture assigns to parents the ultimate responsibility to set standards for their children. Solomon said to his son, "I have taught you in the way of wisdom; I have led you in right paths. When you walk, your steps will not be hindered, and when you run, you will not stumble" (Prov. 4:11–12). Our children's paths will be straighter and smoother if we teach them what is right.

Teach your children to develop self-control

Self-control means to restrain or exercise control over one's impulses, emotions or desires. Aristotle once said, "I count him braver who overcomes his desires than him who conquers his enemies; for the hardest victory is the victory over self." Our greatest enemy is often ourselves, or as the cartoon character Pogo would say, "We have met the enemy, and it is us."

Developing the ability to control our emotions and impulses is one of the most vital issues of the day. Everywhere we turn we see the devastating consequences of people who have given in to their desires with no thought of consequences in the lives of other people. Children are shooting and killing other children over matters that are trivial. In one situation a 10-year-old boy shot and wounded a 13-year-old boy in a disagreement over a dance contest.[2]

Such behavior should not surprise us. Paul warns Timothy that in the latter days men would be "without self-control" (2 Tim. 3:3). We appear to have reached that day. This makes it all the more important that we exercise self-control ourselves and teach it to our children.

Self-control is as much caught as it is taught. That's why it is so important that we parents model the ability to control our impulses. Proverbs urges this temperance when it admonishes, "Have you found honey? Eat only as much as you need, lest you be filled with it and vomit" (25:16).

Teach your children and even your grandchildren the skills of a self-controlled life. Help them to learn how to start something and finish it. Many attics, basements and garages are filled with half-finished projects. Young people are too ready to quit school or a job when they tire of them or encounter their first obstacle. They don't have the stick-to-itiveness that comes with self-control.

My son, Tim, once decided to quit college. He wasn't having trouble with his grades; in fact, he was quite good in school. But it looked to him like school was going to take too much of his time and there were other things in life he wanted to do. Fortunately, his mother and I were able to convince him of the long-term benefits of completing school. Tim finished his degree program, continued for a master's degree and is now working on his doctorate.

Another discipline our children need to learn from us is the consistent study of God's Word. Guide them into developing a quiet time. If you're not sure what study aid to suggest, go to your pastor or your Christian bookstore. Both should be able to suggest material. By studying God's Word your children will come to a greater understanding of the importance of self-control.

Self-control is not repressing our desires in the sense of denying that they exist. It is bringing them out in the open, admitting them to God and seeking His aid in dealing with them. It is refusing to give in to the instinct to do whatever you want.

Lessons to be learned

God's wisdom not only speaks to the things we need to teach our children, it also addresses the things we need to learn as parents so we can teach our sons and daughters more effectively. Much of this wisdom has to do with discipline. Discipline used to be one of the four pillars of the Christian home (along with trust, love and the Bible), but not anymore. The word *discipline* literally means "to teach." We get the word *disciple* (a learner) from the same root. We are good disciplinarians when we are good teachers.

Unfortunately, discipline is absent in many homes. Dr. Benjamin Spock wrote a book several decades ago in which he urged parents to raise their children without discipline—especially spanking. The book caught on (after all, it's hard work to discipline) and generations have been raised based on his theories. Even though today Dr. Spock repudiates most of what he taught earlier, his child-care book still sells half a million copies each year.

With the abandonment of discipline, juvenile delinquency has increased. The American Bar Association says that crimes involving guns, drugs and juveniles are putting an exceptional crunch on the nation's courts. Furthermore, violence and drugs increasingly find juveniles in court as both offenders and victims. In fact, youngsters 12 to 15 are nearly as likely as those 16 to 19 to experience violent crime.[3]

It's time to return to discipline. But it must be discipline guided by God's Word and not the discipline patterned after the theories of fallible men. The late Jacqueline Kennedy was right when she said, "People have too many theories about rearing children. I believe simply in love, security and discipline."[4] That's the biblical way.

We need more parents like the father whose little boy was standing on the porch crying and rubbing his backside. When a kindly, old gentleman walked by, he noticed the boy and asked what the trouble was. "Well," the boy replied, "ever since my daddy lost his psychology book, he's been using his common sense." God's wisdom is common sense wisdom. We have to unlearn the philosophies of the world and get back to God's guide for our life.

Discipline must never be done except in love

Much is being said and written about child abuse today. Hardly a day goes by where you don't find in the newspaper a horror story of a child who was battered or exploited. Children are locked in closets, burned with cigarettes, struck so hard that their bones break or are even killed. That's child abuse, not discipline. Abuse is usually fueled by anger; discipline draws its strength from love.

The Lord does not abuse us, but He does discipline us. Hebrews 12:5-6 says, "My son, do not despise the chastening of the LORD, nor be discouraged when you are rebuked by Him; for whom the LORD *loves* He chastens, and scourges every son whom He receives" (italics mine).

A lack of biblical discipline betrays a lack of love. God's wisdom says, "He who spares his rod hates his son, but he who loves him disciplines him diligently" (Prov. 13:24). The word *diligently* doesn't mean "harshly"; it means "consistently." Why do we find it so hard to be consistent? Perhaps because we think we are doing our children a favor by backing off, by postponing discipline; but just the opposite is true. That only creates confusion. The child, of course, is glad to escape the chastening, but when he breaks the rule again, he doesn't know what will happen. In fact, some children might be encouraged to misbehave again just to find out what will happen.

Maybe another reason for our inconsistency is that we react to our children's misbehavior without the benefit of an established rule of discipline. The child disobeys. We get angry. Our comfort has been disturbed. Our pride is hurt. Our possessions are ruined. Our time is infringed upon. So we retaliate emotionally. That's why it is important to have the rules and the consequences for breaking them agreed upon and understood ahead of time. Consistency provides security and a sense of being loved and cared for, and children thrive on these, even if they don't always like the consequences.

Discipline works, but only if it teaches

Jay Kesler, president of Taylor University, said, "The rules and disciplines of our households should not be aimed at simply keeping control and order. There is more to it all. Rules are teaching tools."[5]

Sometimes when things get out of control at home, we are willing to forgo discipline and settle for some peace and quiet. But that's a short-term solution. God's wisdom says, "Do not withhold correction from a child, for if you beat him with a rod, he will not die. You shall beat him with a rod, and deliver his soul from hell" (Prov. 23:13-14). The ultimate goal of discipline is not to bring order to the chaos of your home; it is to bring your child into a relationship with God the Father that will "deliver his soul from hell."

Discipline that is not a knee-jerk reaction to our pain or embarrassment benefits our children spiritually in a number of ways. If applied consistently, discipline will help keep our children out of some of the deeper pits of sin. Dealing with issues such as stealing, lying or irresponsibility is much easier before your child becomes a young adult. There comes a point when they are less likely to allow us to teach them anything. As Ruth Graham commented, "The time for teaching and training is pre-teen. When they reach the teen years, it's time to shut up and start listening."[6] Teach them right from wrong when they are young; they will need to know the difference all their lives.

Furthermore, consistent discipline teaches that there are consequences for our actions. The need for discipline points out to a young person that he is a sinner. Romans 3:23 says, "For all have sinned and fall short of the glory of God." Our children must know that there are always consequences to sin. Romans 6:23 says, "For the wages of sin is death." This undergirds all that they have learned about actions and consequences. From this point it is just a short step to share the rest of Romans 6:23, which says, "but the gift of God is eternal life in Christ Jesus our Lord."

When children are not disciplined correctly, they think they can get away with their behavior or wheedle their way out of reaping the consequences. When they face God, that won't be possible. We will have taught them the wrong thing.

Discipline reflects a belief both in the sinfulness of humanity and the grace of God

No one has to teach children how to sin. They are born with the innate instinct to get angry and throw their toys. Or to kick and bite in retaliation for being kicked or bitten. Or to throw tantrums and hold their breath. God's wisdom says, "Foolishness is bound up in the heart of a child; the rod of correction will drive it far from him" (Prov. 22:15). David understood this when he said, "Behold, I was brought forth in iniquity, and in sin my mother conceived me" (Ps. 51:5). Discipline is necessary not because we have problem children, but because our children have a problem with sin. Discipline communicates the truth that this is wrong and unacceptable behavior.

But discipline is also an opportunity to demonstrate the grace of God. God disciplines us out of grace because He loves us and wants us to live a life that is unmarred by sin and rebellion as much as possible. Furthermore, when the discipline is over and the lesson is learned, He receives us back to Himself.

The same motive should lie behind the discipline of our children. We need to communicate through our discipline that we don't hate them—and therefore we are punishing them. This is not easily understood and will take a great deal of reaffirming love to convince a whimpering child that you punished him because you love him. But if you want your children to have the happiest and most fulfilling life possible, you must not fail to teach them through discipline. When you discipline them you are removing from their life attitudes or actions that will ultimately endanger their happiness.

What should a parent do when discipline is over? Receive your little one back into your arms again. He needs to be assured that you loved him before he was disciplined, you loved him while was being disciplined and you will love him always.

Discipline teaches us about ourselves

A judge called a young Chicago boy into his chambers. He announced that he had decided to award custody of the boy to his mother. "Oh, no!" cried the boy. "Mother beats me." "Then," said the judge, "I will give your father custody." "Oh, no!" said the boy. "Father beats me too." "Then where will you go?" the judge asked the boy. "Give me to the Cubs," the boy quipped. "They can't beat anyone!"

Beating a child is a serious offense. Abusing a child is a crime. An important caution always must be sounded when we talk about discipline. We are sinners just as much as our children. We need to check our motivation for disciplining. Is it to get even? Is it because we are defending our rights to have peace and quiet or to have a moment to ourselves? When discipline occurs for *our* benefit instead of the child's, we are in danger of moving out of discipline and into abuse.

Discipline is a time for fairness, but not negotiations

A set of parents who had learned tact in dealing with their young son would always ask him at bedtime, "Do you want to go to bed with your teddy bear or your Snoopy?" The boy felt like he was making a choice, but either choice got him to bed, which was the parents' goal. But kids are smart! One evening, before the parents had a chance to pull their usual routine, their son asked, "Shall I stay up and watch the David Letterman show or the Jay Leno show?"

Children are great negotiators. They will try every trick in the book to see if they can out-manipulate you. But parents cannot allow that to happen. God's wisdom says, "A scoffer does not love one who reproves him, nor will he go to the wise" (Prov. 15:12). Expect some resistance, but don't allow your child to control the discipline.

When the child is in control, it teaches him several wrong lessons. He becomes confident that he can talk, cry or lie his way out of any situation. That may work for awhile, but ultimately, either as an adolescent or an adult, it will catch up with him and he will find himself in serious trouble.

Furthermore, it demeans God's honor. God has placed you as a parent at the head of your home. His Word states that children are to obey their parents "in the Lord, for this is right" (Eph. 6:1; see also Col. 3:20). God has a reason for this. Parents are to raise and protect their children. When the children are in control, they end up raising themselves. They make the choices, and no child has the wisdom or experience to make some of the decisions he is faced with. It is not fair to the child nor honoring to God.

If discipline in your home is subject to negotiation, as a parent you will have a tendency to make your discipline unreasonably high. Why? Because you know your child will negotiate you downward. This encourages the inclination to bargain and chips away at your authority. Make your first response be your final response.

That doesn't mean you can't bend a little. There is a big difference between bending and negotiating. Negotiations force you to give in areas that you think are right. On the other hand, if you "bend" the discipline, it is your choice. You are still in control.

In his book *The Enormous Exception,* Earl Palmer noted that the Golden Gate Bridge in San Francisco, which is directly over the San Andreas Fault, is built to sway some 20 feet at the center of its one-mile suspension span. That is one of the secrets to its durability; its flexibility enables it to bend without breaking. Parents need that same flexibility. Rigid family rules sometimes create unfair situations. Those are the times when we need to sway. An extra hour past bedtime, a skipped nap or even a day out of school for a special occasion won't cause serious damage as long as the exception doesn't become the rule.

Think about the discipline you intend to administer before you announce it. This prevents you from overreacting and saying something unenforceable, such as, "You're grounded for a year!" Never set a consequence that you can't or don't intend to carry out. Once you have announced a discipline, don't change it.

Discipline establishes parameters

Parents need to remember that discipline is positive. When God's Word describes family discipline, it says, "My son, give attention to my words; incline your ear to my sayings. Do not let them depart from your eyes; keep them in the midst of your heart; *for they are life to those who find them, and health to all their flesh*" (Prov. 4:20-22, italics mine).

Setting boundaries and enforcing those boundaries through discipline adds to a child's security. A group of educators decided to remove the chain fences from around the school playgrounds. They believed the fences caused feelings of confinement and restraint. But as soon as the fences were removed, the children huddled in the center of the playground to play. The conclusion? Children need to know where the limits are.

As a matter of course, kids will push and prod those boundaries, but that's not necessarily because they want to break them. They may only want to experience the security of knowing that the fence is still there and standing strong.

Discipline brings peace

A cartoon in the *New Yorker* showed a father scowling over a very bad report card while his little boy stood by, asking, "What do you think it is, Dad? Heredity or environment?" It can't be denied that the home environment has a strong influence on academic performance. In fact, there are no areas of a child's life that the home doesn't influence.

Unfortunately, the word that best describes many homes today is *chaotic.* Much of this chaos is caused by a lack of discipline. In speaking of the discipline problems in schools, columnist John Rosemond observed, "The discipline problems in schools come primarily from America's homes. They are a matter of parents who send children to school without the discipline it takes to dig in and get an education; parents who overindulge and undercorrect; parents who neither indulge nor correct . . . parents who expect schools to do what they themselves have been too lazy or busy to do—namely, teach their children the Three R's of respect, responsibility and resourcefulness."[7]

Proverbs 29:17 says, "Correct your son, and he will give you rest; yes, he will give delight to your soul." The word translated "rest" means "to settle down" or "to make quiet." If there is to be peace in our homes, a peace that will transfer to our schools and other places, there must be discipline. *Delight* is the word used for dainty food. One could say that discipline, when it is done in love, makes finger food for the soul. It creates truffles out of terror, cookies out of chaos.

Discipline demonstrates hope

As long as you discipline, you are saying that you believe there is hope to save your child from his own destruction. Proverbs 19:18 admonishes us, "Chasten your son while there is hope." A lack of discipline indicates that the parents have either given up or no longer care. Either case is tragic. One of the saddest things that can happen is for people to give up on us and stop caring what happens to us. The Carnegie Council on Adolescent Development released a study in 1995 that pointed out that "youngsters who have a web of support, especially the active involvement of parents and extended family, will rarely get into problem behaviors that plague a growing number of our young people."[8]

When we give up on our children, we send the message that they are hopeless. Proverbs 19:18 goes on to say, "and do not set your heart on his destruction." To tell our children that we no longer hold out any hope for them, that we have given up on them, is to doom them to fulfill our prophecy. It's hard to believe in yourself when no one else does, especially your parents. On the other hand, as long as we have hope, they will have hope. Discipline is one way to communicate this hope.

Discipline invests in the future

The discipline (or lack of it) imposed today will have a ripple effect. It will affect not only the children whom you discipline but their children and perhaps even their children's children. A good example of this comes from the family of Max Jukes. Mr. Jukes lived in New York during the early 1700s. He was an unprincipled, undisciplined fellow who married a girl of like character. A researcher who traced the descendants of the Jukes family discovered that from this union came 1,026 descendants. Three hundred of them died prematurely. One hundred were sent to the penitentiary for an average of 13 years each. One hundred and ninety were public prostitutes, and 100 were drunkards. While the family made no contributions to society, they did cost the state $1.2 million.

How we discipline and how our children respond to discipline will have an effect for a very long time. Proverbs 13:18 says, "Poverty and shame will come to him who disdains correction, but he who regards a rebuke will be honored."

Get started

The shortest time in the world is the span between your child's birth and when he or she walks out the door as an adult. If you are in the midst of raising children, it may not seem that way now, but just wait. Years from now when you look back on their childhood days, they will seem to have passed by too quickly.

This is why you need to begin to instill God's wisdom into your child today. When I was a young teenager, I watched as the people in our church filed past my father (the pastor) to shake his hand after the Sunday service. On one occasion I watched a little girl about six or seven raise her foot and stomp down on my father's toe as hard as she could. Her mother said, "Oh, dear, I can't wait until she's old enough that I can discipline her. She shouldn't do that." My teen mind said, *Lady, you're already six years too late.*

There's no time like the present to invest in your child's discipline. If your children can learn the alphabet, their colors and to sing along with Barney, then they are not too young to learn right from wrong. Discipline is love; abuse is hate. Make sure you know the difference. Love your child.

One hundred years from now, it will not matter how large your bank account was, what sort of house you lived in or what kind of car you drove. You can be sure the world won't know and won't care. On the other hand, this world may be a different place because you taught your child to choose God's guide for his life's choices.

---

[1] David Swartzlander, "Values without religion," *Lincoln Journal Star*, December 2, 1995, pp. 1D, 3D.

[2] Margaret Reist, "Dance contest led to youth shooting, victim says," *Lincoln Journal Star*, December 13, 1995, p. 1A.

[3] "Crime rate crushing courts," *Christians & Society Today*, December 1994.

[4] "Women's Words," *Indianapolis Star*, March, 12, 1995, p. J4.

[5] Jo Berry, *Proverbs for Easier Living* (Minneapolis, Minn.: World Wide Publications, 1980), p. 113.

[6] Ruth Graham, *Homemade*, Vol. 16, No. 11, November 1992.

[7] John Rosemond, "Lack of discipline starts at home but becomes evident in schools," *Lincoln Journal Star*, November 30, 1995, p. 2D.

[8] John Brandon, "The positive influence in a child's life," *Indianapolis Star*, November 10, 1995.

Chapter 8

Wisdom and Your Relatives

A poor man is shunned by all his relatives.
Proverbs 19:7

Almost everyone has a full complement of relatives. There are relatives we dearly love, relatives we can barely stand and relatives we hardly know. But no matter how we feel about them, we have to learn to deal appropriately with our kith and kin. God's Word gives us the wisdom to know how to rightly treat these people who are related to us.

Our required relatives

You have no choice about some relatives; you are born with them. Take your parents, for example. As you go through various stages in your life, your attitude towards your parents varies. Mark Twain said of his father, "When I was a boy of 14, my father was so ignorant I could hardly stand to have the old man around. But when I got to be 21, I was astonished at how much the old man had learned in seven years."

Since our parents are living longer, we have more time to be "astonished." The *Oxford Book of Aging* says, "For the first time in human history, most people can expect to live into their 70s in reasonably good health, and those over age 85 are the fastest-growing group in our population."[1] Demographer James Vaupel and colleagues at Duke University say that the number of people in industrialized nations age 100 or older generally has doubled every decade since 1950. At the beginning of this decade there were 3,890 people 100 years old or older in England and Wales; 3,477 in France; 26,869 in Japan; 2,540 in West Germany; 1,646 in Italy; 1,108 in the Netherlands; 583 in Sweden and 507 in Australia.[2]

This growing pool of older people means more couples are seeing their parents live into these advanced years. About the time the average, middle-aged couple is sending their last child off to college or into the job market, they are faced with a new challenge— to be parents to their parents. God's Word gives us guidance for even this situation.

Aging parents need special respect

Parents deserve to be treated with respect, especially when they are elderly. God's Word says, "The eye that mocks his father, and scorns obedience to his mother, the ravens of the valley will pick it out, and the young eagles will eat it" (Prov. 30:17). While they no longer exercise the same authority over us as when we were children, aging parents are not to be treated irreverently.

There is a Mexican legend about a man who did not want to be burdened with his feeble, old father. He asked his young son to take the old man to a mountain cabin and leave him there with food and a blanket. The boy returned with half the blanket. The father wanted to know why he brought half of the blanket back with him. The young boy replied, "I am saving this for you, Father."[3] The respect we show our parents will eventually come back either to bless or haunt us.

Be sensitive to how others treat your parents as well. Old age should be a time of respect, not a time of discourtesy. One woman shared how a doctor who examined her mother kept addressing his remarks to her instead of to her mother. After a while, the elderly woman became irritated and interrupted the conversation to ask, "Doctor, do you do crossword puzzles?" "Yes," the man replied. "Do you do them in pencil or ink?" Uncertain as to where this conversation was leading, the doctor decided to humor the woman, so he replied, "In pencil." Looking him right in the eye, the spunky lady said, "Well, I do mine in ink. Now talk to *me!*" The doctor got the message: aging parents deserve respect.

Aging parents need special attention

Growing older has a significant impact on the human body. Your heart muscle is about 30 percent less efficient at age 80 than it was when you were 29. In the years between ages 30 and 75, the body may lose 20 to 30 percent of its cells. These microscopic alterations collectively produce significant changes in the body's tissues and organs. As the years go by, food doesn't taste as good. Our taste buds, scattered over the surface of the tongue, normally last only a few days and are replaced. As we age, however, this replacement slows down until the taste buds are lost faster than they can be replaced. By age 75, a person has lost up to 64 percent of his or her taste buds. Even the sense of smell is duller.

Someone suggested that if you want to know what it's like to grow old, smear dirt on your glasses, stuff cotton in your ears, put on heavy shoes that are too big and wear gloves. Then try to spend the day in a normal way.

We children of older parents need to be reminded that our folks need special attention in their later years. Old knee and hip joints don't work the way they once did. Some parents need help getting in and out of bed and getting to church, grocery stores, banks, doctor's offices as well as a multitude of other places.

This takes time, energy and maybe rearranging your schedule. It may even seem more demanding than you think reasonable, but just remember how many sporting events, parties, trips to school, etc., your parents worked into their schedule for you. This is a small repayment for the love and care they gave during your adolescent years.

Aging parents need special understanding

Someone joked, "Just about the time your face clears up,

your mind goes fuzzy." But aging doesn't always have a negative affect on mental ability. Physician Alex Comfort says, "The human brain does not shrink, wilt, perish or deteriorate with age. It normally continues to function well through as many as nine decades."[4] The unprecedented rise in nontraditional students (students returning to the classroom after an extended absence of years) at colleges and universities is an indication that cognitive abilities do not necessarily fail as we grow older. One example is Florence Nagamoto of Oakland, California, who received her associate of arts degree on the same evening she celebrated her 80th birthday.[5]

But many of us have seen age take a toll in the mental deterioration of our parents. Some researchers claim that the speed at which our minds process new material (called Fluid Intelligence or thinking ability) declines with age, even though the acquisition of knowledge through schooling or everyday experience is unaffected. Some elderly people contract diseases that attack the brain and damage the ability to reason and remember. One of the most devastating is Alzheimer's disease: up to 2 million Americans are affected, and the vast majority are older than 60. Alzheimer's begins with memory loss for recent events and progresses to the point that the victim cannot recognize family members or remember his or her name.

All of us who minister to elderly parents must remember that they do not think as clearly or rapidly as they once did. Explanations may take longer and reminders might be needed more frequently. You may hear the same story several times in one day, but the men and women who taught you your ABCs and tied your shoes still deserve your special understanding. God will give you that understanding if you ask Him for it.

Aging parents need special grace

Grace means "unmerited favor" or an "exemption from judgment." As our parents get older, we will find more and more occasions to extend that kind of grace. As they age, people sometimes become more cranky and irritable. Some become demanding even to the point of being unreasonable. Unreasonable demands need to be met with reasonable and gracious responses.

One anonymous person recognized these possibilities and wrote this prayer,

> Lord, thou knowest better than I, that I am growing older, will someday be old. Keep me from getting talkative, and particularly from the fatal habit of thinking I must say something on every subject and every occasion. Release me from craving to try to straighten out everybody's affairs. Make me thoughtful, but not moody, helpful, but not bossy. With my vast store of wisdom, it seems a pity not to use it all, but thou knowest, Lord, that I want a few friends left at the end of life. Keep my mind free from the recital of endless details; give me wings to get to the point. Seal my lips on my aches and pains. They are increasing and my love of rehearsing them is becoming sweeter as the years go by. I ask for grace enough to listen to the tales of others' pains. Help me endure them patiently. Teach me the glorious lesson that occasionally it is possible that I may be mistaken. Keep me reasonably sweet; I do not want to be a saint; some are very hard to live with, but a sour old person is one of the crowning works of the devil. Help me to exact all possible fun out of life. There are so many funny things around us and I don't want to miss any of them.[6]

When you are tempted to grow impatient with their sometimes childish behavior, remember the years you inflicted your parents with your own childishness. By grace they continued to love you, and now, by grace, it is your opportunity to return the favor.

Aging parents need special support

Many elderly parents need not only emotional and physical support but financial support as well. The costs of long-term care continues to escalate at an alarming rate. From 1993 to 2018, the number of elderly in nursing homes will jump 64 percent, while those in home care will increase by 42 percent. Spending for this long-term care is expected to soar by 120 percent— to $168.2 billion— during this same time period. [7]

Add to this the prospect of cuts in future Social Security benefits, increases in co-payments for health care and an ever-expanding cost of living, and you have the ingredients for a fiscal fiasco. Obviously, a lot of elderly parents cannot make it on their own without some help. As we give to missions, to building funds and to many other good causes, it is appropriate that our parents also should benefit from our finances.

The apostle Paul declares, "But if anyone does not provide for his own, and especially for those of his household, he has denied the faith and is worse than an unbeliever" (1 Tim. 5:8). God takes seriously the need to care for those in our family, including our aging parents.

Jewish scholar and philosopher Abraham Heschel noted, "The test of a people is how it behaves toward the elderly. It is easy to love children. Even tyrants and dictators make a point of being fond of children. But the affection and care for the old, the incurable, the helpless, are the true gold mines of a culture."[8]

The most important relatives we adults have (apart from our children) are our mothers and fathers. Proverbs says, "Listen to your father who begot you, and do not despise your mother when she is old" (Prov. 23:22). Let's treat aging parents with the wisdom found in God's Word.

Our acquired relatives

Marriage is not only between two people but also between two families. When we marry, we acquire a whole new set of relatives. Whether we call them "in-laws" or "out-laws" depends on how well we apply God's wisdom.

We need to treat them justly

Nothing creates tension as quickly as when one set of in-laws feels they are being neglected in favor of the other. And what is the most common barometer used to gauge this perceived neglect? Holidays!

Some families value certain holidays more than others, but the "big four" for American families are Thanksgiving, Christmas, Easter and the Fourth of July. These are special times when the absence of family members is particularly noticed. How should couples deal with the conflicting demands placed upon them during these times? It isn't easy.

My wife and I were born and raised in the same town. Although we lived hundreds of miles away from our parents, each Thanksgiving, Christmas or other holiday we were together presented quite a challenge. We had to split our time with each family. Thanksgiving meant two turkey dinners. At noon I would hear, "Eat, eat." Only hours later, in the words of Yogi Berra, it was *deja vu* all over again. But we never allowed our mothers to think we did not appreciate all the work they put into setting their banquet tables. We were fair with both families.

God's wisdom says, "A false balance is an abomination to the LORD, but a just weight is His delight" (Prov. 11:1). Make sure you approach your family obligations with the justice of God's wisdom.

We need to treat them honestly

In-laws may be the most difficult people for us to be honest with. The English language is filled with euphemisms for dishonesty. When confronted about lying, many people euphemistically say they are only "bending" or "stretching" the truth. *The Day America Told the Truth* reports that 91 percent of Americans lie routinely; 36 percent of those confess to dark, important lies; 75 percent lie to friends; 73 percent lie to siblings; 69 percent to spouses. No wonder we feel inclined to use euphemisms— the truth is too convicting.[9]

No matter what euphemism we use, however, dishonesty will catch up with us. We may find ourselves in the same predicament as Joe the butcher. Just as he was ready to close, Mrs. Brown, one of his best customers, came in and asked for a nice roasting hen. Joe put the last one he had on the scales. "It's 2 pounds, 4 ounces— that will be $2.25." Mrs. Brown thought it was too small and inquired, "Do you have a larger one?" Joe went to the cooler and returned with the same chicken. Weighing it, he said, "This one is 3 pounds, 2 ounces. That will be $3.12." Still not convinced it would feed her hungry family, Mrs. Brown said, "I think I'll take them both!" You can imagine the damage Joe's lie caused to his relationship with Mrs. Brown. It will do the same with your in-laws. The worst way to improve in-law relations is to be caught stretching the truth with them.

In-laws are our parents too. We need to love them and treat them as honestly as we do the rest of the world. If we borrow money, we should repay it promptly within the set time limit; if we make a promise, we should keep it at all costs; if we borrow a tool, we should return it in good condition. Sometimes people are tempted to "shade the truth" with their in-laws to make it appear their son or daughter got quite a deal in his or her marriage. But the fact that we are related by marriage does not give us the right to treat in-laws less honestly than we treat anyone else.

Proverbs says that God is "a shield to those who walk uprightly" (2:7). No such promise applies to those who deal dishonestly with their in-laws.

We need to treat them kindly

Kindness should be the rule in every relationship. Unfortunately, when it comes to our in-laws, it isn't always practiced. Mother-in-law jokes are an example.

I wonder how many mothers-in-law in real life silently suffer under the unkind treatment they receive at the hands of stand-up comedians or on T.V. sitcoms? Seldom are mothers-in-law cast in a favorable light. On the other hand, the insights of a mother-in-law are not always right. Benjamin Franklin's mother-in-law hesitated letting her daughter marry a printer because there already were two printing offices in the United States, and she feared that the country might not be able to support a third. Harry Truman's mother-in-law recommended he not waste his time seeking re-election as president of the United States. Since we all make mistakes, it isn't fair to hold these errors against mothers-in-law more than we would against anyone else.

God's wisdom says, "Let not mercy [kindness, NASB] and truth forsake you; bind them around your neck, write them on the tablet of your heart, and so find favor and high esteem in the sight of God and man" (Prov. 3:3-4).

It's a fact of life. When you choose a spouse, you get in-laws in the bargain. Friends may come and go, but in-laws are with you for a lifetime. Your spouse is the beneficiary of their years of struggle and hard work. Your children become their pride and joy. Your spouse's siblings sometimes become your dearest friends and most ardent supporters. Doesn't such potential deserve to be nurtured in God's wisdom? Don't just make the best of in-laws; make friends with them. Help them appreciate you by appreciating them.

Our spiritual relatives

Christians belong to yet a third family— the family of God. When we receive Christ as our Savior, God adopts us (Rom. 8:15). In the process we gain a new life, a new hope and a new set of relatives.

Often we view our spiritual relatives as less important than our biological relatives, but God does not. Galatians 6:10 says, "Therefore, as we have opportunity, let us do good to all, *especially to those who are of the household of faith*" (italics mine). Our responsibilities to brothers and sisters in Christ are no less important than the ones we have toward our relatives by birth or marriage.

We need to treat them compassionately

These are difficult days. Many people cannot afford to carry medical insurance. Others have lost their jobs through downsizings or plant closings. Some of our Christian brothers and sisters are sitting next to us in the pew wondering if they can make the next house payment. Elderly members of our congregation on fixed incomes may be going hungry. What does God's wisdom say our response should be?

In the New Testament, James writes, "If a brother or sister is naked and destitute of daily food, and one of you says to them, 'Depart in peace, be warmed and filled,' but you do not give them the things which are needed for the body, what does it profit?" (James 2:15-16). To claim that the saving grace of the Lord Jesus Christ fills your heart and then not respond with compassion to those in need is inconceivable. Salvation is not earned by works, but it is supposed to work!

In the Old Testament, giving to those with special needs was considered to be of special merit. The law required that the gleanings of the field, the olive tree and the vineyard should be left for the poor, such as the fatherless and the widow, and the sojourner (Lev. 19:9-10; 23:22). Deuteronomy admonishes us, "For the poor will never cease from the land; therefore I command you, saying, 'You shall open your hand wide to your brother, to your poor and your needy, in your land'" (15:11).

God's wisdom says that your spiritual life is impacted by your dealings with those in need, especially our fellow believers. "He who despises his neighbor sins; but he who has mercy on the poor, happy is he" (Prov. 14:21). To turn your back on your neighbors (Jesus defines a neighbor as anyone in our presence who has a need—Luke 10:30-37) is blatant sin.

Proverbs 19:17 says, "He who has pity on the poor lends to the LORD, and He will pay back what he has given." The idea of "lending" to the Lord implies repayment. The repayment does not come from the person who received our gift but from God Himself. Since you can be sure that God will not be indebted to any man, the time will come when He will return the payment with interest.

In the 1800s, both Charles Spurgeon and George Mueller had ministries that supported orphanages. During a time of financial need, Spurgeon came to Bristol, England, to raise £300 to support his work with homeless children. Having succeeded in reaching his goal, however, he felt the Lord prompting him to give the money to George Mueller's orphanage. Spurgeon's first response was to resist the idea, but when he realized this prompting was of the Lord, he gave in. Returning home empty-handed, Spurgeon went to his study to open his mail. In a letter that had come during his absence was a check for more than the amount he had given his Christian brother, George Mueller.

We have no guarantees that God's return on our investment will be monetary. We do know, however, that it is impossible to out-give God and that the man who lends generously to God is rewarded handsomely by Him.

We need to treat them tactfully

Some of the most sensitive individuals find their way into the church. Without a great deal of tact, it is easy to bruise egos and wound spirits. Apparently this is nothing new. The apostle Paul urged Timothy, "Do not rebuke an older man, but exhort him as a father, the younger men as brothers, the older women as mothers, the younger as sisters, with all purity" (1 Tim. 5:1–2). In other words, we should be as sensitive and caring with our relatives in the church as we ought to be with our relatives at home.

The hurts that Christians receive from other Christians can mar them for life. One denominational leader shared that the most distressing part of church fights is that unkind words and deeds are remembered long after the issue that caused the fight is forgotten. An old wrangler explained that when a group of thoroughbred horses is attacked, they stand in a circle facing each other and, with their back legs, kick at the enemy. Donkeys do just the opposite; they face the enemy and kick each other! It's too bad that Christians act more often like donkeys than thoroughbreds.

Sometimes a lack of tact has left the Body of Christ badly splintered. The late J. Vernon McGee suggested the following change in the words of "Onward, Christian Soldiers":

> Like a halting caravan, moves the church of Christ;
>
> We are feebly faltering toward our timid tryst.
>
> We are all divided, many bodies we,
>
> Kept apart by doctrine and lack of charity.
>
> Careful Christian pilgrims! Walk in doubt and fear,
>
> With the cross of Jesus, bringing up the rear.

I'm sure Dr. McGee wasn't suggesting that we give up exhorting one another. The wisdom in Proverbs says, "As iron sharpens iron, so a man sharpens the countenance of his friend" (Prov. 27:17). But it must be done graciously and diplomatically, or the result will be a church "all divided . . . kept apart by doctrine and lack of charity."

When you encounter sensitive individuals in your church who need biblical exhortation or instruction, be tactful. They are your brothers and sisters in the Lord. God's wisdom says, "Whoever guards his mouth and tongue keeps his soul from troubles" (Prov. 21:23). Say what must be said, but say it with tact!

Rejoicing in your relatives

Someone jokingly said the hardest thing to disguise is your true feelings when you put your relatives on the plane for home. If we follow God's Word, however, we won't have to worry about disguising our feelings. They will be appropriate feelings of compassion and respect. When we exercise godly wisdom, our relatives will be people we can enjoy and cherish.

If you haven't done so in a long time, make it a point to pray for your relatives—blood relatives, in-laws and Christian brothers and sisters. It's hard not to appreciate people you pray for. You may find yourself enjoying them even more once you have invested some of your prayer life in them. That's a choice you won't regret making.

---

1 *Oxford Book of Aging*, quoted by George Sweeting in "Aging Well," *Moody*, July/August 1995, p. 62.

2 Alan L. Otten, "People Patterns," *The Wall Street Journal*, January 27, 1995, p. B1.

3 Anna B. Mower, *So Who's Afraid of Birthdays?* (Philadelphia: Trumpet Books, 1969), p. 114.

4 Dennis Coon, *Introduction to Psychology, 5th ed.* (St. Paul, Minn.: West Publishing Co., 1989), p. 407.

5 Annie Nakao, "On 80th birthday, artist gets her degree," *Electronic San Francisco Examiner*, November 16, 1995, via the Internet.

6 Charles Swindoll, *Strike the Original Match* (Minneapolis, Minn.: World Wide Publications, 1980), p. 189.

7 Annie Nakao, "Running on empty," *Electronic San Francisco Examiner*, April 4, 1995.

8 Abraham Heschel, *Homemade*, Vol. 17, No. 2, February 1993.

9 James Patterson and Peter Kim, *The Day America Told the Truth* (New York: Prentice Hall, 1991), pp. 45–46. Quoted in *USA Today*, January 9, 1992, p. 4D.

Chapter 9

Wisdom and
Your Friends

A friend loves at all times.
Proverbs 17:17

Paul Simon, of the singing team Simon and Garfunkel, wrote of the American soul when he penned the lyrics to the popular song "I Am a Rock." In it he sang, "I have no need of friendship. Friendship causes pain."

These sentiments seem true of the Western world and especially the United States. Author Vance Packard called Americans "a nation of strangers." Louise Bernikow, another author, calls loneliness "an American epidemic." Increasingly, we interact more with television, computers and even banking machines rather than with live people. It's little wonder that loneliness is a growing problem. Thomas Wolfe wrote, "The whole conviction of my life now rests upon the belief that loneliness, far from being a rare and curious phenomenon, peculiar to myself and a few other solitary men, is the central and inevitable fact of human existence."[1]

This feeling is perhaps understandable if you are elderly and all alone, but age seems to make little difference in the degree of loneliness one experiences. Guy Doud, 1986 Teacher of the Year, talks about the surprising number of high school students who mention in their papers the struggle they have with loneliness. A study by the American Council of Life Insurance reported that the most lonely group in America is college students. The young are not immune to the pain of loneliness.

Fame is no deterrence either. During Elvis Presley's last engagement at the Las Vegas Hilton in December 1976, he kept a pad by his bed on which he wrote down his thoughts. One of the cleaning staff found a personal note he had written and then thrown away in the wastebasket. It said:

> I feel so alone sometimes. The night is quiet for me. I'd love to be able to sleep. I am glad that everyone is gone now. I'll probably not rest. I have no need for all this. Help me, Lord.[2]

Loneliness seeps under the doors of the famous and through the window sills of the wealthy and affluent just the way it does with everyone else. It plays no favorites and cannot be bought off.

Even busyness is only a temporary stopgap. One busy executive described it like this:

> There it is again! A twinge of pain? Forget it. It will go away. In the business of my day, I've places to go and things to do. A round of meetings with entrepreneurs. Planes to catch and taxis to hail. I have life by the tail. But what is this painful wail? From the depths of me I ache. It greets me when I wake. Even in a crowded room of people I can hear a haunting toll from the church bell steeple. There's nothing wrong with me. I'm a success, as anyone can see. I, I hurt. I feel an emptiness. This feeling, is it loneliness? Loneliness? I'm married with children, three. Yet at times I feel so alone.[3]

If youthfulness is no solution, fame is futile and busyness provides no lasting immunity, what is the answer to loneliness? God's answer is friends. Friends cheer our day with little deeds of thoughtfulness. They speak words of comfort when we need to hear them most. They often are God's hands and feet, and sometimes His mouthpiece as well, to meet our needs and soothe our fears. Friends stand by us when everyone else has given up and gone home. Aristotle once defined a friend as one soul in two bodies.

Friendship is vital in our struggle against isolation and loneliness. That's why we should be concerned when George Barna noted in his Barna Report for 1994–95 that 29 percent of his respondents indicated that they were spending less times with friends.[4] If this trend is not reversed, loneliness will continue to grow. A friend was important to God (James 2:23); how much more important should he be to you and me? Let's consider what the wisdom of Proverbs advises us about developing friendships.

Proverbs' Ten Commandments of Friendship

Perhaps we can best remember God's foundations of friendship by expressing them in ten commandment form couched in the words of old English.

1. Thou shalt not choose thy friends on superficial grounds.

Sometimes we choose to build friendships for shallow reasons. As Proverbs 19:6 reminds us, "Many entreat the favor of the nobility, and every man is a friend to one who gives gifts." While many of us may not be crass enough to seek someone's friendship because of his power or because of the gifts we might receive from him, there are other superficial reasons for choosing friends.

Perhaps we choose to build a friendship with another person because he is close in age. This isn't entirely wrong, of course, but limiting our circle of friends based on age means we lose the wisdom that someone older might provide or the enthusiasm and fresh insight that someone younger might bring into our lives. Age should not be the only determining factor of friendship.

When I was just 24 years old, I was a professor at a Bible college. Some of my students were older than I was. The college provided a duplex for my family and me. Above us lived another professor and his wife, Urban and Beulah Cline. They were more than 30 years older than I, yet they became fast friends to Linda and me. It was one of the most rewarding friendships I have had, even though the age difference was significant. Don't shortchange yourself by making friends solely in your age group.

Other times we choose friends because we work with them or they are in the same profession we are. When this happens, we are prone to talk shop even on social occasions— which is unfair for our family members. A friend knows who you are, understands who you have been and accepts who you are becoming. You cannot achieve this depth of friendship by limiting your discussions to work-related subjects. This is also true if all you talk about is sports or (as is common among Christians) church. These topics are fine, but a real friendship has to go beyond superficial matters.

Some people choose friends for the social benefits the friendship might bring. Such a friendship is not only superficial, it is dishonest. Ulterior motives never make a good foundation for a relationship of any kind, and friendship is no exception. Proverbs 19:4 says, "Wealth makes many friends," but we must never forget that a friend who can be bought also can be sold.

None of these are sufficient reasons for making a person your friend. A friendship should be made because it can make both of you better people. As someone has said, "Don't choose friends by what they can do for you but for what you can do for each other." Proverbs say, "As iron sharpens iron, so a man sharpens the countenance of his friend" (27:17). Don't choose friends to form a mutual admiration club; rather, choose friends for mutual edification. Often you can handle the truth if someone who cares for you tells it to you. A caring friend may be the only one who will tell you what you need to hear.

Another good reason for choosing a friend is that he shares your purpose in life. Does your friend's mission statement read nearly the same as yours? It should. In the Book of Amos, the Lord asks, "Can two walk together, unless they are agreed?" (3:3). The implied answer is no. If you select a friend who is headed in a direction different from what God wants for you, you will have to disappoint one or the other. Either you will follow your friend and disobey God, or you will obey God and likely lose your friend. Choosing friends who have the same spiritual agenda as you saves you from this dilemma.

Another excellent reason for choosing a friend is that he builds you up spiritually. Everyone is moving in his spiritual life. If you aren't moving forward, you are slipping backwards. You need to pick a friend who will keep you going in the right direction—forward.

Jerry McAuley spent seven years in Sing Sing prison for stealing and counterfeiting. It was there he received Christ and eventually got his life together. When he got out of prison, he started America's first skid row mission in New York City. He became a friend to the worst criminals and nefarious characters of his day, always pointing them toward Christ. Shortly before his death, he told his wife, "I know that soon tuberculosis will take my life, but I want to die on my knees, still praying for the lost. I'd rather have some poor soul that I led to the Lord put one small rose on my grave than to have the wealth of a millionaire."

His wish was granted. At Jerry McAuley's funeral, an aged, shabbily dressed man appeared. Handing one of the ushers a few flowers, he asked him in a voice trembling with emotion to place them on the coffin. Then he said apologetically, "Jerry was my friend. I hope he will know that they came from old Joe Chappy."

2. Thou shalt recognize the incredible influence friends have on you.

No one can avoid being influenced by those we care about. This is why we must choose our friends carefully. A *Peanuts* cartoon showed Peppermint Patty talking to Charlie Brown.

She said, "Guess what, Chuck. The first day of school, and I got sent to the principal's office. It was your fault, Chuck." The round-headed little guy said, "My fault? Why do you say everything is my fault?" Peppermint Patty replied, "You're my friend, aren't you, Chuck? You should have been a better influence on me." While there's a pound of false blame being dished up, this cartoon also reveals an ounce of truth. God's wisdom says, "He who walks with wise men will be wise, but the companion of fools will be destroyed" (Prov. 13:20).

Our friends have significant influence on us. Gospel pianist Tedd Smith used to say, "To learn to appreciate beauty, keep looking at it. To gain an appreciation of good music, keep listening to it. To appreciate poetry, keep reading it. Taste is formed by what you live with." The more you keep company with your friends, the more they will either build you up or tear you down. The old country adage is right: "If you lie down with the dogs, you'll get up with the fleas."

Sometimes friends influence us without our even knowing it. An industrial company in a small town wanted the city fathers to make certain concessions before it would expand its operation. Some residents believed the company was of no special benefit and the town would get along just as well without it. The company thought otherwise. To make its point, the company began paying its employees in silver dollars instead of issuing checks. Silver dollars, which had been rare up until then, began to pour over the counters in stores, filling stations, theaters and refreshment stands. It became evident that the company had much more influence on the town than people realized, and opposition to the expansion was quietly withdrawn.

Never underestimate the influence of your friends. Quietly, consistently, almost imperceptibly, they can have a lasting influence on your life.

3. Thou shalt not pick fights with thy friends.

This may seem like common sense, but surprisingly, this wisdom is often not followed. God's Word says, "Do not strive with a man without cause, if he has done you no harm" (Prov. 3:30). Failure to heed this advice usually results in one of two consequences: you will grow either to like one another or dislike one another. Sometimes in the stormy exchange of ideas, an appreciation for your friend's individuality will surface. Even though you don't agree with him, you appreciate the fact that he stands up for what he believes. The more likely result, however, is that you will come to dislike one another and distance yourself from each other.

There may be legitimate reasons for not getting along with a friend. Sometimes friends we make as children change as they get older. They may choose a different path than ours. They may come under the influence of others and be led into areas that we know are wrong. You will want to share your concern, even try to dissuade them from the path they have chosen, but if they adamantly oppose what you say to them, sometimes you simply have to let go. As the apostle Paul says, "If it is possible, as much as depends on you, live peaceably with all men" (Rom. 12:18). When it is not possible, be pleasant, be kind, be loving, but when the time comes, be gone.

Picking fights with friends only causes harm. It prevents both of you from experiencing harmony. In musical terms, harmony is a combination of different notes that sound good together. A chord adds richness and depth to the music by blending different sounds. That's God's plan for friends—two people blending their differences together to add richness to their lives. Psalm 133 describes it this way:

Behold, how good and how pleasant it is
for brethren to dwell together in unity!
It is like the precious oil upon the head,
running down on the beard, the beard of Aaron,
running down on the edge of his garments.
It is like the dew of Hermon,
descending upon the mountains of Zion;

for there the LORD commanded the blessing—
life forevermore.

It would be a shame to miss such blessing because of a quarrel!

But fighting with your friend does something even more sinister. It destroys trust. Samuel Johnson observed, "There can be no friendship without confidence, and no confidence without integrity." Integrity means being true to your word. To pick a frivolous fight with a friend ruins his confidence in you, and consequently your integrity with others.

Max Lucado tells the story of two friends fighting side by side in battle. The combat was ferocious, and one of the two young soldiers was wounded. When the troops pulled back, this fallen soldier could not return to the trenches. Against his officer's orders, his friend went back to get him. He returned mortally wounded, and his friend, whom he had carried back, was dead. The officer looked at the dying soldier, shook his head and said, "It wasn't worth it." Hearing the remark, the young man smiled and said, "But it was worth it, sir, because when I got to him he was still alive and he said, "Jim, I knew you'd come."[5] These friends knew what it meant to trust each other. We should be trustworthy and choose friends who return the favor.

If you want to keep your friends, don't pick fights with them. If you do, your friends will wish they had chosen their friends more carefully.

4. Thou shalt be understanding to thy friends at all times.

Patience and friendship are synonymous. No good friendship lacks patience; some great friendships require great patience. George Washington said this about friendship:

Be courteous to all, but intimate with few, and let those few be well tried before you give them your confidence. True friendship is a plant of slow growth, and must undergo and withstand the shocks of adversity before it is entitled to the appellation.[6]

Sometimes we try to hurry friendships to make them blossom faster than our friends want. Yet Washington was right when he described friendship as "a plant of slow growth." When we try to rush what normally takes time, we become frustrated and sometimes hinder the growth in the process. We're like the little boy who planted seeds in his garden and then went out every day and uncovered them to see if they were growing. His impatience actually inhibited their growth. Another great American, Ben Franklin, advised, "Be slow in choosing friends and be even slower in leaving them."[7] Good friendships deserve time to mature properly. Make sure you allow enough time.

During the process of growing a friendship, be willing to overlook faults and shortcomings. Proverbs says, "The discretion of a man makes him slow to anger, and his glory is to overlook a transgression" (Prov. 19:11). A critical spirit comes naturally to many of us. We allow what's wrong to overshadow what's right. We're much like the group of people who were shown a white piece of poster board with a small dot in the middle. When asked what they saw, everyone replied, "A black dot." The person conducting this experiment then pointed out that the white poster board was more than 50 times the size of the dot, but people saw only the dot. Sometimes our friend's strengths are 50 times greater than his weaknesses, but we see only the weaknesses.

To overlook a transgression means you never retaliate. If your friend forgets to send a birthday card to you, do not neglect to send a card to her. It also means you refuse to remember ills that your friend may have committed against you. Furthermore, if you need to make restitution to your friend, do so even if he is unwilling to make restitution to you. You are not responsible for your friend's actions—only for yours.

Proverbs 20:3 says, "It is honorable for a man to stop striving, since any fool can start a quarrel." If any fool can start a quarrel, it must take a wise man or woman to stop one. Perhaps you are facing this choice between foolishness and wisdom right now. Opt for the wisdom. Be understanding to your friend.

5. Thou shalt be available to thy friends when they need you.

Real friends are there when you need them. They bear your sorrows and celebrate your joys. They slap you on the back at birthday parties and embrace you at funerals. Sharing is an intrinsic part of friendship. Proverbs 18:24 says, "But there is a friend who sticks closer than a brother." Ultimately, of course, this verse refers to the Lord Jesus. He is the friend who said, "I will never leave you nor forsake you" (Heb. 13:5). But we, too, must stick close to our friends. We must be there when they need us.

In his book *Loving God*, Charles Colson relates the story of Jack Swigert and Bill Armstrong. Swigert had piloted the Apollo 13 lunar mission in 1970. He was now in the oncology unit at Georgetown University Hospital. Cancer was waging its final assault on his body.

With the dying man was a quiet visitor, sitting in the spot he had occupied almost every night since Swigert was admitted. The man was Bill Armstrong, U.S. Senator from Colorado and chairman of the Senate subcommittee handling Washington's hottest issue, Social Security. He was one of the busiest and most powerful men in Washington, but as a committed Christian and Jack Swigert's friend, he was fulfilling a responsibility he would neither delegate nor shirk.

That night he leaned over the bed and said quietly, "Jack, you're going to be all right. God loves you. I love you. You are surrounded by friends who are praying for you. You're going to be all right." Bill pulled his chair closer to the bed, opened his Bible and began to read, "The Lord is my shepherd, I shall not want. . . ."

Time passed. As Bill began to read Psalm 150, Jack's ragged breathing stopped. He knew there was nothing more he could do. His friend was dead.

Politicians are busy people, especially Senate subcommittee chairmen. Yet it never occurred to Bill Armstrong that he was too busy to be at the hospital. There was nothing dramatic or heroic about his decision—just a friend being there when he was needed.[8]

That's the kind of friend God's wisdom says we should be. Whether we can do something or not is immaterial. Just being there to console with our presence and our prayers is enough.

6. Thou shalt encourage thy friend, for someday thou shalt need encouragement thyself.

The Boston Marathon is among the world's best-known races. Perhaps the most infamous portions of this 26-mile, 385-yard course is what has endearingly become called "Heartbreak Hill." There, along where the course winds itself up the hill, thousands of spectators gather. They stand and cheer as they see weary runners about to collapse. During the marathon a few years ago one young man was near total exhaustion as he approached the foot of Heartbreak Hill. It looked like he would be unable to go a step farther. But about halfway up the hill an older runner, who was obviously in better shape, came alongside the younger man, put his arm around him and spoke quietly to him. Together, step by step, they painstakingly made their way up the hill.

That's how the wisdom of God sees us relating to our friends. Proverbs 12:25 says, "Anxiety in the heart of man causes depression, but a good word makes it glad." You and I are called to offer that word of cheer when our friends feel they cannot go another step. When they are depressed, discouraged, perhaps even at the point of despair, it is both our responsibility and privilege as Christian brothers or sisters to encourage and comfort. The famed actress Celeste Holm once observed, "We live by encouragement and die without it—slowly, sadly, and angrily." That should never happen to any of our friends.

Real friends build up their friends. You can do that by having a Bible study with them. Share the good news with your friend; help him find God's answers for life's problems. It will be a source of encouragement for both of you.

Another way to build up your friend is to attend a Bible conference together. I know a man and his wife who attend a Bible conference each year and always invite another couple to join them. At a conference where I was speaking last year, they invited a husband and wife who did not know Christ as their Savior. They told me what they had done, and we began to pray that God would save their friends. Throughout that week I had several opportunities to talk with this couple about their need to commit their lives to the Lord. Before the week was over, God convicted them of their sin, they opened their hearts to Christ and became a part of God's family. But this would never have happened had it not been for one couple who encouraged another couple by inviting them to the conference.

God wants us to invest ourselves in our friends and be an encouragement to them. If we invest in stocks and bonds that someday will no longer be of use to us, why not invest in those with whom you can spend eternity in heaven?

7. Thou shalt not withhold good from thy friend.

Friendship is a lot like a bank account: you need to put some money in before you can draw some money out. We need to invest in our friends if we expect to receive back. No one appreciates a friend who constantly takes without giving something in return.

Some friends are like the stingy man who went Christmas shopping for a gift to send to a friend out of state. He scoured the malls for something cheap but found nothing until he came across a vase with a broken handle. Because of the damage, the shop had reduced the price drastically and the man bought it. When the clerk offered to wrap the gift, the man agreed and then mailed it to his friend, figuring he would think it had been broken in transit. A week after Christmas he received this note: "Thank you for the lovely vase. It was so nice of you to wrap each piece separately."

Selfishness is never blessed by God. Proverbs 3:27 says, "Do not withhold good from those to whom it is due, when it is in the power of your hand to do so." We owe our friends the best we can provide. Whether it is with our time, emotions or money, if we can help our friends, God's wisdom says we are obligated to do so.

While I was in seminary I pastored the First Baptist Church in Middleboro, Massachusetts. The church was made up of some wonderful people. In spite of all my mistakes as a young pastor, they graciously remained my friends. The church was small and couldn't afford to pay me much, but they were sensitive to that and did the best they could. One of the families in the church kept some chickens around their farm. Every Sunday night, week after week, when I came out to my car after the evening service, on the front seat there would be two dozen eggs and a freshly dressed chicken. Those two dozen eggs and that chicken, along with my small paycheck, kept our family going for the rest of the week.

Those dear folks did what they could. They did not withhold the good that they could do from their friend. When it was in their power, they shared with my family and me. That's what friends do.

8. Thou shalt not demand thine own way with thy friends.

One of the characteristics of love as described in 1 Corinthians 13 is that it "does not seek its own" (v. 5). Proverbs puts it this way: "A man who isolates himself seeks his own desire; he rages against all wise judgment" (18:1). The New International Version says, "An unfriendly man pursues selfish ends; he defies all sound judgment." A friendship is doomed when one or both of the friends insists everything be done his or her way.

There's an old fable about a man who gratefully arrived in heaven and told the Lord how glad he was to be there, but he had one small request. He wanted to take a peek into hell so he could better appreciate heaven. The Lord granted his request. When he looked into hell, the man saw a long table loaded with all kinds of delicious food. Oddly, everyone at the table appeared to be starving to death. Confused, the man asked, "Lord, I don't get it! With all that food, why are these people starving?" "That's simple," the Lord replied, "each one is required to take food from the table with four-foot chopsticks, which are too long to reach their own mouths." Turning away from hell and looking around him, the man noticed the same arrangement in heaven except everyone looked well fed. What was the difference? The Lord explained, "Here people can't feed themselves, so they feed each other."

Although this is just a fable, it does illustrate the need for our concern to be aimed toward our friends and not toward ourselves. We all need to be like Timothy, whom Paul described as one "who will sincerely care for your state. For all [except Timothy] seek their own" (Phil. 2:20–21).

Perhaps the best way to be a good friend is to be a loving friend. In his book *Dream a New Dream*, Dale Galloway tells the story of a shy, quiet boy named Chad. One day Chad came home and told his mother he wanted to make a valentine for everyone in his class. Her heart sank. *I wish he wouldn't do that*, she thought, because she had watched how other children treated him when they walked home from school. They laughed and hung on to each other, but Chad was never included. He was always a few yards behind them. Nevertheless, Chad's mom bought the paper and glue and crayons he would need to make the valentines. Night after night for the next three weeks Chad painstakingly made his valentines until all 35 were done.

Valentine's Day dawned. Chad was beside himself with excitement. He put his precious valentines in a bag and bolted out the door. His mom knew he would be disappointed, so she baked some cookies to help ease the pain. It hurt her to think that Chad wouldn't get many valentines—maybe none at all.

That afternoon she heard the children outside. Sure enough, they were laughing and having the best time. And, as always, there was Chad in the rear. His hands were empty and she fully expected him to burst into tears as soon as he came inside. When the door opened she choked back the tears and said, "Mommy has some warm cookies and milk for you." Chad hardly heard her words. He just marched right on by mumbling, "Not a one, not a single one." Her heart sank until she listened more carefully and heard Chad say, "I didn't forget a one, not a single one!" Chad wasn't into friendship for what he could get out of it; he was into friendship for what he could give to it. His heart pounded with satisfaction and his face gleamed with joy. He hadn't forgotten a single friend.

Do you want to have strong friendships? Then learn to give a little and love a lot. If we learn to think about others instead of ourselves, we will have a friendship that doesn't demand its own way.

9. Thou shalt be open and honest with thy friends so they will be open and honest with thee.

Being open and honest is risky business, especially if what you have to share is not complimentary. But God's wisdom calls us to be exactly that with our friends. Proverbs 27:5-6 says, "Open rebuke is better than love carefully concealed. Faithful are the wounds of a friend, but the kisses of an enemy are deceitful."

This doesn't mean we tell our friends every little thing they do wrong. That's being picky, not honest. Some people seem to gravitate toward the negative. They have the gift of telling it like it is. But Proverbs 27:5-6 does not give us the right to declare an open season on our friends. On the other hand, it does tell us that if we truly love our friends, we will lovingly, yet firmly, confront them when their behavior is less than Christian.

When I was a college president, a young student became a good friend of mine. One day, however, he seriously broke the campus code of conduct, and I knew I had to expel him. In fact, his infraction was so serious, as president of the college I had to ask him to leave the campus immediately. But he had no place to go. As his friend, I invited him to come to my house to spend the night. Being open and honest doesn't mean you always destroy a friendship. Handled properly, confrontation can deepen your friendship.

When Christ confronted the woman caught in adultery, He treated her with respect, which was more than she deserved. He helped her save face and maintain her dignity. He called her "woman," not "prostitute," "tramp" or other derogatory terms. He told her, however, that what she was doing was wrong and then sent her away to repent and do an about-face in lifestyle (John 8:3-11). The implications are that she did. But through it all, Jesus was able to maintain the attitude of a friend, not of a judge or an executioner.

You cannot help your friends by closing your eyes to their sins. Proverbs 27:6 says it is "deceitful" to do so because by your silence you are giving approval to something you know is wrong. It is better to speak up and take the chance of being misunderstood than to remain silent and see your friend go to rack and ruin. If you expect your friends to be honest with you, you have to be honest with them.

10. Thou shalt not wear out thy welcome with thy friends.

Even the best of friends need breathing room. Some people are honest enough to tell you, "I need my space." A few people need lots of space, others just a little. But everyone needs some. That's why God's wisdom says, "Seldom set foot in your neighbor's house, lest he become weary of you and hate you" (Prov. 25:17). One way to determine how much time you should spend at a friend's house is to watch how much time he spends at yours. This will give you some idea of how much "space" he or she needs.

Proverbs also tells us, "He who blesses his friend with a loud voice, rising early in the morning, it will be counted a curse to him" (27:14). In other words, be sensitive to the needs and habits of your friends. Some people are morning people— early to bed and early to rise. Others think morning begins around lunchtime. They prefer the late hours on both ends of the day. Respect these differences in your friends. If you do not, you may find your welcome becoming a little worn.

The best way to have a friend is to be a friend. The best way to keep a friend is to give him the distance and privacy we all need at times. Prying into your friend's business is a sure way to ruin a friendship. This is also true of family friends. If a mother wants to be the best friend of her daughter, she must learn not to demand all her daughter's time and force her interests on her daughter. That may be the kind of behavior some girls expect from a mother, but it's not the kind of behavior they expect from a friend.

We all need friends

Someone said, "No man is so wealthy that he doesn't need friends." Friends cannot be calculated in terms of dollars and cents.

When World War I ended, the king and queen of Belgium wanted to honor President Woodrow Wilson for all the help he had given their country. They offered him the top three medals of honor in Belgium, but he turned them all down, saying, "I did only what any other person would have done in my position." Not to be denied, the king and queen made a new order to which Wilson alone belonged. They called it, "The Friend of the Belgium People." President Wilson accepted it. He could turn down a medal, but he couldn't turn down friendship.

If you need a friend, remember that in Christ you have a friend who "sticks closer than a brother." Enjoy the company of the best friend you can ever have. But don't exclude the company of all your other friends. Pray that God might send a special friend across your path. Such a friend can enrich your life as perhaps no family member ever can. "Better is a neighbor nearby than a brother far away" (Prov. 27:10). The right friend can bless your life and make your life a blessing to God. Ask Him to provide that kind of friend for you.

---

[1] Thomas Wolfe, *You Can't Go Home Again* (New York: Harper, 1940).

[2] *USA Today*, April 17, 1992, p. 2D.

[3] Ken Olson, *Hey man! Open Up & Live* (New York: Fawcett, 1978), pp. 147-148.

[4] George Barna, *Virtual America* (Ventura, Calif.: Regal Books, 1994), p. 42. Barna also noted that 23 percent indicated they were spending more time with their friends, for a net loss of 6 percent.

[5] Max Lucado, *On the Anvil* (Wheaton, Ill.: Tyndale House, 1985), pp. 114-115.

[6] Barbara Milo Ohrbach, *A Token of Friendship* (New York: Clarkson N. Potter, 1987), p. 4.

[7] Lucado, *Anvil*, p. 115.

[8] Charles Colson, *Loving God* (Grand Rapids, Mich.: Zondervan, 1983), pp. 131–132.

Chapter 10

Wisdom and Your Purity

With her flattering lips she seduced him.
Proverbs 7:21

If you are married, are you committed to a monogamous relationship with your spouse? Christians who allow God's Word to guide their life's choices are. Remaining sexually pure and faithful to your spouse is the moral, biblical and spiritual plan of God for your life. But did you also know that faithfulness in marriage is beneficial in other ways? According to a study done by the Population Association of America, the lifetime commitment that comes with marriage reduces stress, improves health and increases wealth. Married couples are financially better off because they are more likely to pool and invest their money. Married men also tend to make more money than single men, which means less stress and better medical care.[1]

If marriage is such a wonderful institution, then why are so many marriages falling apart today? Why are so many men and women falling for the seduction of other people?

In a survey conducted by *Psychology Today* magazine, one-third of the married men and women questioned said they have had at least one extramarital affair. *USA Today* readers, responding to a "Living in the USA" survey, indicated that approximately one-third (39 percent of men, 27 percent of women) have had an extramarital affair.

Many theories have been offered for this disheartening trend. Perhaps the most unique one is given by Anglican bishop Richard Holloway from Edinburgh, Scotland.

According to the bishop, adultery is in the genes. God made us to be adulterers, and we should not condemn people for following their instincts.[2] That may be the bishop's answer, but it is not God's answer.

The real reason so many people, including Christians, are falling into the sticky web of seduction is that they do not take seriously God's Word to guide their actions. People often don't recognize how real the danger is until it's too late. That's why you and I need to know what God's wisdom says about how to identify seduction and protect ourselves against it.

Seductive character

In the Book of Proverbs, Solomon casts the role of the seducer as a woman in order to parallel wisdom, who also is cast as a female. In real life the seducer could just as easily be a male. Seduction is not a matter of who we are but what we are. Scripture says that those who engage in seduction are fools (Prov. 9:13). This means that they are:

Stubborn

Fools, including seductive fools, resist every attempt to enlighten themselves and reverse their foolishness. God's wisdom says, "A fool has no delight in understanding, but in expressing his own heart" (Prov. 18:2). Such willfulness caused Solomon to exclaim, "How long, you simple ones, will you love simplicity? For scorners delight in their scorning, and fools hate knowledge" (Prov. 1:22).

During the 18th century, Dr. Johann Beringer was a professor of natural philosophy at the University of Wurzburg in Germany. Dr. Beringer adamantly maintained that fossils were capricious fabrications of God. His students decided to play a trick on him, so they made and buried in a nearby hill hundreds of clay tablets supporting this theory. One of these pranksters even made a tablet that appeared to be signed by God Himself.

The professor was so convinced of his "find" that he published a book on the subject, repeatedly ignoring the confessions of his students. He thought they were trying to rob him of the glory of his theory. It was not until he discovered tablets bearing his own name that he realized the hoax. No wonder God's wisdom says, "The way of a fool is right in his own eyes, but he who heeds counsel is wise" (Prov. 12:15).

Fools endure much tribulation because of their stubbornness. Proverbs 10:13 says, "Wisdom is found on the lips of him who has understanding, but a rod is for the back of him who is devoid of understanding." Again, God warns, "For the turning away of the simple will slay them, and the complacency of fools will destroy them" (Prov. 1:32). Stubbornness is the fruit of foolishness.

Selfish

Fools are not only stubborn, they are selfish as well. This is one of the reasons why fools fall to seduction so easily. The fool has no room in his heart for anyone but himself. He is so wrapped up in his own desires that he is oblivious to the people whom he hurts. God's wisdom acknowledges this when it says, "Fools mock at sin, but among the upright there is favor" (Prov. 14:9). The Hebrew word translated in this verse as "sin" (*asham*) literally means "guilt" or by implication "a fault." When the fool looks at his guilt, he refuses to take it seriously.

The New International Version translates Proverbs 14:9, "Fools mock at making amends for sin, but goodwill is found among the upright." God's Word says of the seductive fool, "This is the way of an adulterous woman: She eats and wipes her mouth, and says, '*I have done no wickedness*'" (Prov. 30:20, italics mine). There is no recognition of sin. Making amends is deemed unnecessary, silly and moralistic by the fool.

When a young man said to his pastor, "I don't think I am a sinner," the preacher asked if he would be willing for his mother to know all he had done or said or thought, all his motives and all his desires. After a moment's thought the young man said, "No, I certainly would not like to have them known, not for all the world." A moment's reflection revealed how foolish he was. The beginning of wisdom is the "fear of the LORD" (Prov. 9:10), which reveals our sinfulness. Anyone who will not recognize his or her sin is a fool.

No self-control

Proverbs 9:13 says, "She is simple, and knows nothing," or, as the NIV translates it, "she is undisciplined and without knowledge." A lack of discipline or self-control is behind the majority of our moral problems today. An undisciplined thought life leading to undisciplined behavior is the weak link in the chain protecting us from seduction.

The seducer is not a thinker; he or she is a reactor. Do you ever feel an urge for something inappropriate and instinctively respond to meet it? If so, God's wisdom says you are a fool. Samson was that way. He could strangle a lion but could not strangle his desires for a Philistine woman. He was able to burst the fetters of his enemy, but he could not break the cords of his own lusts. He had the courage to burn the crops of others but did not have the courage to quench the burning in his flesh for the seductress Delilah. Responding to every instinctive urge of our body without the self-control of a mind informed by the wisdom of God is like stepping on a banana peel. It will cause you to fall every time.

Self-control is a declining commodity in American society. What began as a suggestion from a fast-food chain that "you deserve a break today" has culminated in the feeling that we deserve whatever we want (or whoever we want), when we want it. Instant gratification is the watchword of our generation.

Sadly, we don't know what's good for us. In 1900 the ten leading causes of death were 1) pneumonia and influenza; 2) tuberculosis; 3) intestinal ulcers; 4) heart disease; 5) stroke; 6) kidney disease; 7) accidents; 8) cancer; 9) senility and 10) diphtheria. In 1993 the top ten causes of death were 1) heart disease; 2) cancer; 3) strokes; 4) lung disease;

5) accidents; 6) pneumonia and influenza; 7) diabetes; 8) HIV; 9) suicide and 10) homicide.[3]

All the major causes for death in the early 1900s were either accidents or health-related. Today, three out of the ten major causes of death are frequently related to man's failure to exercise self-control: HIV, suicide and homicide. The character of the seductive person perfectly fits our society. He is stubborn, selfish and lacks self-control.

Seductive behavior

Harvard University did a study some years ago on the subject of nonverbal communication. The research revealed that there are more than 700,000 different ways to communicate without words.[4] Long before we can determine their character, seductive fools make themselves known by their behavior. They are not lights hidden under baskets. They make plain by their actions what kind of people they are. The behavior of the seductive person is:

Boisterous

God's wisdom describes the seductress this way: "She was loud and rebellious, her feet would not stay at home" (Prov.7:11). This woman was no wallflower. She displayed an air of self-confidence. On the surface she seemed happy and looking for a good time.

Many men find this appealing— especially those whom the Bible calls "simple." This doesn't mean simpleminded or mentally challenged. The Hebrew word translated "simple" comes from the root word *pathah* (paw-thaw), which, in this context, means to be "open" or "roomy" in a moral sense. They have no strict or narrow standards of conduct for the people they associate with. They are open-minded, non-judgmental, real 90s kind of guys. God's wisdom says this kind of a man takes the path to the seductive woman's home (Prov. 7:7-8). God's wisdom also says he is a fool.

For the seducer, this boisterousness is actually a cover for rebelliousness. Actions that would be resented if done in a serious manner are often accepted if done in the name of having fun. Who wants to be a wet blanket? Don't take offense; take advantage. A good party in most societies usually involves at least two ingredients: alcohol and immorality. Getting drunk is such a common expectation that during the Christmas holidays, when numerous parties are given, some cities offer free taxi rides home to those too inebriated to drive. Along with alcohol and merriment comes immorality. With the loosening that comes from liquor, it's a short step from flirtation to fornication. With just a little alcohol, the inhibitions come down and people indulge in fleshly sins that they would be far more reticent to commit in a more sober state.

Don't be fooled. In the midst of unrestrained boisterousness, the seducer has ample opportunity to exert his or her influence.

Aggressive

The seducer is not a stay-at-home kind of woman. She is always on the prowl. Like a lion seeking whom it may devour, the immoral person is not content to wait. Instead, she seeks out places where victims might be found. God's wisdom says, "At times she was outside, at times in the open square, lurking at every corner" (Prov. 7:12). Today, bars and parties are the concourse of seduction. When a likely prospect comes near, the trap is sprung. Proverbs 7:13 says, "So she *caught* him and kissed him" (italics mine).

The seductress is blatant about her aggressive hunt for sex. Hers are not idle words when she tells the young man, "So I came out to meet you, diligently to seek your face, and I have found you" (Prov. 7:15). No hunter every planned his hunt more carefully.

Furthermore, seductive people can appear in almost any setting. A few years ago, a pastor friend and I missed our flight from Amsterdam to Athens and had to spend the night in the Dutch capital. While walking from the train station to our hotel, to our amazement, there were dozens of prostitutes on display, each seated in a large picture window, calling out to the people as they walked by. One could literally window shop, and many men were.

You and I can never let our guard down. Seductive people show up in the least expected places. It may be at the office Christmas party, at a neighborhood gathering or the community swimming pool. They are aggressively looking for people to seduce. Don't let them take you by surprise.

Appealing

The seducer makes things as appealing as possible. The seductress in Proverbs 7 tells her intended victim, "I have spread my bed with tapestry, colored coverings of Egyptian linen. I have perfumed my bed with myrrh, aloes, and cinnamon" (vv. 16-17). This woman had taken every measure to make her bedroom enticing. She appealed to every sense.

By nature you and I are sensual creatures— God made us that way. He gave us eyes to behold beauty, a nose to detect aromas and ears to react to sounds. In addition, He gave us nerve endings all over our body to respond when touched or stroked. But what God has given us to make life more pleasurable, Satan uses to entrap us. What was provided as a good gift can become chains of bondage if we aren't careful.

Sexual fantasies can be as appealing and seductive as the real thing. Each month, 18 million men in the United States buy one or more of the 165 different pornographic magazines; one in every ten American men reads *Playboy*, *Penthouse* or *Hustler* on a monthly basis.[5]

In 1994, Archibald Hart, dean of the School of Psychology at Fuller Theological Seminary, published *The Sexual Man*, a study of sexual attitudes and experiences among 600 "religious" men. Nearly 75 percent of the men who grew up in religious homes said that they had been exposed to pornographic material before age 15. Such is the aggressive appeal of seduction.

The men in this sample firmly believed that pornography is bad: 80 percent said that it degrades women, 58 percent said that it promotes violence against women, 82 percent said it distorts sexuality, and 71 percent said it is destructive. In addition to their overwhelmingly negative view of porn, 70 percent of these same men said pornography is addictive.[6]

It's ironic, isn't it, that something so appalling is also so appealing? But that's the nature of seduction: if it were not so appealing, we wouldn't have a problem with it. If you think you are safe from the appeal of seduction or that you are too spiritual or too old to fall victim to the appeal of seduction, you are only fooling yourself.

Seductive talk

Seductive talk is quite common today. You hear it on the television, around the office and at other social functions. It is filled with double meanings and innuendos. Never underestimate the power of words to influence your behavior. George Sweeting wrote, "The tongue is powerful! The eloquence of Bernard of Clairvaux was so great that thousands of people felt compelled to leave their earthly goods behind them and join Europe's Second Crusade. The rousing delivery of Patrick Henry's immortal words, 'Give me liberty or give me death!' inspired the struggling colonies to fight on and secure their national liberty. Who today will ever forget the stirring words of the young president, John Kennedy, 'Ask not what your country can do for you— ask what you can do for your country.'"[7] The power of seductive talk is equally great as the power of an inspiring call to arms.

The seductive person has many tools with which to ply his or her trade, but one of the most powerful is the tongue. Seductive words can appear as:

Sweet words

A sugar coating conceals the taste of a bitter pill. The seducer covers his dastardly deeds with a sweetness that often disguises the foulness of what he is proposing. Male and female seducers alike use such sugary words. Proverbs 5:3 says, "For the lips of an immoral woman drip honey." Honey was the sweetest substance known in Solomon's day.

The woman of Proverbs 7 says, "Come, let us take our fill of love until morning; let us delight ourselves with love" (v. 18). All is sweetness and light. She makes no mention of her vows to her husband, which would be broken. She has no concern for the possible destruction of her family, nor thoughts of the extended family (aunts, uncles, parents, grandparents) who would be hurt by this illicit relationship. Neither is she concerned with the example she is setting for the younger generation. All of this is far from her mind. Even more tragic, it is far from the mind of the one she seduces as well.

If you have ever watched daytime soaps on television, you are familiar with this seduction. On TV and in the movies men and women are constantly bed-hopping with seemingly no concern for the consequences. There is no mention of sexually transmitted diseases, no talk of illegitimate pregnancies, no loss of self-respect. Television and the movies claim to reflect life as it really is, but that's a lie. Such portrayals project an unrealistic view of life. The consequences of living the lifestyles of the rich and famous may better be described as living the lifestyles of the rebellious and foolish. Hollywood only shows the sugar coating; you never see the bitter pill afterwards. We need to be smarter than to believe what Satan says is true. The great seducer is the father of lies.

Seduction leaves wounds and broken lives that are difficult to heal. It destroys marriages, families and children. Little wonder that a third of U.S. teenagers (a group that is especially susceptible to this lie) say they have considered suicide, 15 percent have thought seriously about it, and 6 percent have actually tried, according to a Gallup Poll. The National Institute of Mental Health claims that suicides by 15- to 19-year-olds, which have tripled in the past 30 years to 10 per 100,000, are the second-leading cause of death for that group.[8]

Whatever sweet words you are listening to, from whatever sweet lips, stop and think a moment. No amount of pleasure is worth destroying your family, your spouse, your children and yourself. Seduction may have a happy beginning, but it never has a happy conclusion. Sweet words lead to bitter endings.

Smooth words

Not only are the words of a seducer sugarcoated, they are as smooth as a lake-washed stone. Proverbs 5:3 says, "And her mouth is smoother than oil." The word here translated "smooth" (*chelquah*, khel-kaw) is translated in Proverbs 7:21 as "flattering" lips. Solomon draws a picture of an oily-lipped flatterer whose goal is to slip her words past your reason and into your heart. Most seductresses are very good at this.

It's hard to resist flattery if it's done smoothly. Some people actually court it. The brilliant physician and writer Oliver Wendell Holmes Sr. loved to collect compliments. When he was older he indulged his pastime by saying to someone who had just praised his work, "I am a trifle deaf, you know. Do you mind repeating that a little louder?"

The seducer, however, has a more sinister goal than just to pay an overinflated compliment. He or she desires to drag his victim down into the smooth web of sin and deceit. The one who listens to such seduction will find his feet slipping on a well-oiled slide that leads to personal destruction.

Don't let smooth words grease your path to sin. You wouldn't believe everything an enemy said about you, would you? Remember, you don't have a greater enemy than Satan's seducer who is out to flatten you, not flatter you.

Shameless words

In Birmingham, Alabama, prison officials are issuing hot-pink uniforms for male inmates who are habitual problems. The goal is to shame them into changing their ways.[9] Unfortunately, no such program is available for seducers.

Instead, they shamelessly maintain their innocence. As Agur the son of Jaketh says, "This is the way of an adulterous woman: She eats and wipes her mouth, and says, 'I have done no wickedness'" (Prov. 30:20).

People who have no shame about what they do— who are driven by greed and personal lusts— destroy all that is good in the world. Adulteresses and adulterers certainly are guilty of this destruction, and yet they maintain they have done nothing wrong. They have no regard for the broken lives their sin leaves behind.

Some seducers enter our homes under the harmless guise of entertainment. Much of television is that way. TV critic Robert Feeder of the *Chicago Sun Times* noted that on one day, Oprah Winfrey explored the subject "Should Teens Have Sex at Home?"; Sally Jesse Rafael focused on the children of sexaholics; Geraldo Rivera hosted potential victims who pleaded, "If he gets out of jail, he's going to kill me"; and Joan Rivers dished up soap opera dirt and examined infertility. At the same time, their producers argued that they were responding to what stay-at-home women wanted to see. The sad truth is they may be right. The minds of women especially are being seduced by the shameless words they hear daily on the tube.

Think about this for a moment. Ten years ago, would you have put up with what you watch frequently on TV today? Likely not, but today most viewers, even Christians, are not shocked into shame anymore. We live in a shameless society, which, if we do not follow God's wisdom, will soon become a shockless society. What will be left? After we have done it all and seen it all, what more can we do or see?

Avoiding the trap

Some people would have us think that, given the permissive society in which we live, falling into the trap set by the seducer is inevitable. But if you think that, you are more influenced by the world than you are informed by God's

Word. Wisdom is skillful living in a world that is no friend of God. If you use God's Word to guide your actions, the Bible promises, "When wisdom enters your heart, and knowledge is pleasant to your soul, discretion will preserve you; understanding will keep you, to deliver you from the way of evil, from the man who speaks perverse things" (Prov. 2:10-12).

Even the siren call of the seductress can be silenced. By the power of the Spirit of God living within you, it is possible for you to say no to the sweet, smooth, seducing words of that person who is the greatest temptation in your life. Proverbs 2:16–17 assures you that God's wisdom is able "to deliver you from the immoral woman, from the seductress who flatters with her words, who forsakes the companion of her youth, and forgets the covenant of her God." Your failure is not inevitable; rather, it is quite avoidable.

Successfully avoiding the seducer requires that you:

Use common and moral sense

These are not the days for us to be gullible. Americans have been through a parade of crises in recent years that have shaken our trust: Watergate, Iran-Contra and Whitewater, to name just a few. Consequently, there is a growing skepticism directed primarily at politicians and others in leadership positions. In some cases, that skepticism is healthy.

This same healthy skepticism needs to be aimed at those who come to us with seductive behavior and words. Ask yourself the legitimate questions of Proverbs 6:27-29: "Can a man take fire to his bosom, and his clothes not be burned? Can one walk on hot coals, and his feet not be seared? So is he who goes in to his neighbor's wife; whoever touches her shall not be innocent."

Common sense tells you that you cannot keep an illicit relationship hidden for long. There are too many ways to be found out: a suspicious spouse, a slip of the tongue, bumping into someone you know, an inexplicable bank withdrawal. The question is not *if* the relationship will be discovered, but *when.*

When the inevitable happens, the consequences are destructive. Fred Humphrey, past president of the American Association for Marriage and Family Therapy, points out that about half of married couples either divorce or separate when one spouse learns of the other's affair. Others anguish over trying to salvage the relationship. "Learning about it results in instant pain and anger," he says. "Then there will always be a barrier, to some extent." Perhaps you or someone close to you has already run face first into that barrier. Anyone with common sense should use it to avoid such a destructive situation.

Use your head. You cannot play with fire and not get burned. You cannot listen to smooth, seductive words and not get sucked in. You cannot hang around the places where seductive people can be found and not expect them to assume that you are looking to be seduced. In fact, that's exactly what you are doing. Common sense says if sin is there, get out of there. The Bible says that too (2 Tim. 2:22).

Think before you act

Since you may encounter the seducer at any bend in the road, plan ahead before you confront a seductive situation. Work out in your mind how you will handle it. Know what you will say and do when you confront someone who has designs on seducing you. This is why you memorize Scripture. This is when you need Scripture to reinforce your decision. Proverbs 9:17-18 is one possibility: "Stolen water is sweet, and bread eaten in secret is pleasant. But he does not know that the dead are there, that her guests are in the depths of hell."

Remember this promise from God: "No temptation has overtaken you except such as is common to man; but God is faithful, who will not allow you to be tempted beyond what you are able, but with the temptation will also make the way of escape, that you may be able to bear it" (1 Cor. 10:13). The way of escape may just be the Scriptures you call to mind when you feel your common sense is giving way.

When you think through the consequences of giving in to the seducer, when you know ahead of time what to do and say, the seducer loses his or her great advantage— surprise. Don't expect in the heat of the moment to think rationally and logically; you won't. In the moment of temptation you will be thinking with your lustful flesh, not with your spirit. Do your thinking when you have the luxury of time and reason on your side. Prepare for your encounter with temptation. It may change the result.

Commit yourself to your spouse

A young boy returned from Sunday school, where the Ten Commandments had been the topic, and asked his father, "Daddy, what does it mean when it says, 'Thou shalt not commit agriculture'?" There was hardly a beat between the question and the father's wise reply: "Son, that just means that you're not supposed to plow the other man's field."[10] This man obviously had given some thought to the ways of the seductress before he would have the misfortune of encountering her. He also had reflected thoughtfully on his relationship with his wife and made a commitment to be faithful.

God's wisdom says, "Drink water from your own cistern, and running water from your own well. Should your fountains be dispersed abroad, streams of water in the streets? Let them be only your own, and not for strangers with you. Let your fountain be blessed, and rejoice with the wife of your youth" (Prov. 5:15-17). This is a poetic way of saying what we all know is God's plan for every godly man: you are to have sexual relations only with your wife. You are to enjoy the intimate experience only with your wife and not someone else's wife. You are not to be out fathering children all over town but only in your household. Your thirst is to be quenched only by your wife. If the men of the nation would allow God's wisdom to guide their actions in this regard, we could abolish many of the abortion mills, welfare programs and orphanages that dot our national landscape.

It's time, men, that we take responsibility for our actions. The seductresses are out there and looking for us. But that's because they know many men are looking for them. Stop the demand and the supply will dry up. Don't blame your weakness on the seductress's beauty. The wisdom of God condemns her smooth words and seductive ways, but it also condemns your insatiable thirst for the illicit.

Guard your heart

One of the best known stories that illustrates how the sweet, stolen water of adultery invariably turns bitter is the tragedy of Camelot. In this tale, the marital relationship between King Arthur and Queen Guenevere is trespassed upon when the most trusted knight in the realm, Lancelot, slips his toe across the boundary. It started with a look— an innocent look, without premeditation or evil intent. But it was a short step from a look to lust, from infatuation to infidelity. The look eventually led to a touch. The touch sometime later led to a kiss. The kiss, to adultery. And adultery, to tragedy.

The story of Camelot is repeated in real life almost daily with only minor variations. Lonely women are looking for more than their tired husbands have to offer them. Lecherous husbands are looking for something more exciting than what their wives offer them. The result is a match made in hell— a foolish seductress seducing a foolish seducee.

A man wrote to Ann Landers:

> Eleven years ago, I walked out on a 12-year marriage. My wife was a good person, but for a long time she was under a lot of stress. Instead of helping her, I began an affair with her best friend.

This is what I gave up:

1. Seeing my daughter grow up.

2. The respect of many long-time friends.

3. The enjoyment of living as a family.

4. A wife who was loyal, appreciative and who tried very hard to make me happy.

This is what I got:

1. Two step-children who treated me like dirt.

2. A wife who didn't know how to make anything for dinner but reservations.

3. A wife whose only interest in me was how much money she could get.

4. A wife who disparaged my family and ruined all my existing friendships.

5. Finally, the best thing I got was a bitter, expensive divorce.

Ann, tell your readers that anyone who is married and has his or her next mate all lined up is looking for trouble. People don't know what they are giving up until they no longer have it. Then it's too late.

— Otis of Wisconsin[11]

Otis was living the nightmare that is the result of sin. This nightmare has visited almost every home in America in one way or another. It's the common story of these waning years of the 20th century.

But Otis's story need not be your story. Guard your heart. Make sure no seductive words pierce the seat of your emotions. Guard your mind. Do not think about someone seductively, even for a minute. It has been said that the mind is the most powerful sexual organ of the body. You cannot dwell on sexual thoughts and be impervious to seduction. And guard your eyes. Even the venerable Job, in his old age, said, "I made a covenant with my eyes not to look lustfully at a girl" (Job 31:1, NIV). That's the kind of common sense wisdom we need, and it's the kind that we get from the Book of Proverbs, God's guide for life's choices.

Frequently I am asked what the greatest, most pressing need of the church is for today. Is it revival? Does the church need to be revived? Yes, it does, but that's not our greatest need. Is it evangelism? Does the church need to finish the task of world evangelism? Yes, it does, but that's not our greatest need. The greatest, most pressing need of the church today is the need for purity. We must guard our purity and use God's Word as a guide in doing so. Fervor lost can be regained. Wisdom lost can be regained. But purity lost is gone forever. We can be restored after we have sinned, but we can never again be blameless.

Only God can guard your purity. Give your life to Him, your heart to Him, your thoughts to Him, your dating life to Him, your sexuality to Him, your purity to Him. Let Him guard you through His loving holiness and guide you though the wisdom of His Word.

---

[1] "Marriage is (almost) bliss," *U.S. News & World Report*, April 24, 1995, p. 16.

[2] Paul Majendie, "Bishop blames adultery on 'promiscuous genes,'" *Electronic San Francisco Examiner*, May 17, 1995, via the Internet.

[3] "By the numbers," *U.S. News & World Report*, August 28/September 4, 1995, p. 83.

[4] Tim Hansel, *When I Relax I Feel Guilty* (Elgin, Ill.: David C. Cook/Chariot, 1979), pp. 51-52.

[5] John Crewdson, *By Silence Betrayed: Sexual Abuse of Children* (New York: Harper & Row, 1988), p. 249.

[6] Rob Reynolds, "Breaking Free," *Moody*, March 1994, p. 14.

7 George Sweeting, *How to Resolve Conflicts* (Chicago: Moody Press, 1973), p. 75.

8 Karen S. Peterson, *USA Today*, April 2, 1991, p. 1A.

9 Associated Press, "Problem inmates to be dressed in pink uniforms—for shame," *Lincoln Star*, May 19, 1995, p. 1A.

10 *Reader's Digest*, July 1979, p. 87.

11 "Ann Landers," *Columbus Dispatch*, September 28, 1991, p. 2E.

Chapter 11

Wisdom and
Your Words

A soft answer turns away wrath.
Proverbs 15:1

On the first day of school, some children were asked to tell what their fathers did for a living. One little boy said, "My father writes words on a piece of paper, calls it a poem and gets paid $100." The class was impressed.

The next child said, "That's nothing! My father writes words on a piece of paper, calls it a song and gets paid $1,000."

A third youngster then spoke up, "My father writes words on a piece of paper, calls it a sermon, and it takes four people to collect all the money!" These children are just beginning to learn the power of words.

Words can bring blessings, but they also can bring tragedy. On March 6, 1995, a segment of *The Jenny Jones Show,* a popular television talk show, dealt with "Men Who Have Crushes on Other Men." John Schmitz, 24, did not know when he agreed to appear on the show to meet a "secret admirer" that his admirer was another man. Schmitz was uncomfortable and obviously embarassed to hear an acquaintance, Scott Amedure, 32, proclaim publically that he had a crush on him. Three days later Amedure was found shot to death in his mobile home. Police have charged Schmitz with the crime.

Someone said, "Having a tongue is like having dynamite in your dentures." The only way to control such power and its potential for good and evil is by heeding Scripture. God's guide for life's choices tells us how to govern our tongue and control our words.

Words come in all shapes and sizes. Some are hurtful; some are helpful. Choosing the right ones is critical.

Hasty words

The Book of Proverbs mentions just two things for which there is less hope than for a fool. One is conceit. Proverbs 26:12 says, "Do you see a man wise in his own eyes? There is more hope for a fool than for him." The other is hasty words. Proverbs 29:20 asks, "Do you see a man hasty in his words? There is more hope for a fool than for him."

Like arrows from a bow, words once spoken cannot be recalled. Apologies sometimes don't make up for the hurt caused by hasty words. God's wisdom says, "A brother offended is harder to win than a strong city, and contentions are like the bars of a castle" (Prov. 18:19). Hasty words cheat the mind, betray the heart and ruin a life. There is but one cure for hasty words— always take your time before you respond.

Hasty promises

We live in an era of telemarketing technology. People seeking funds for their causes don't have to go door-to-door anymore. Phone solicitors are able to reach us in the inner sanctum of our homes. Everyone has answered a ringing telephone only to find a person at the other end wanting us to pledge to some worthy cause. How can we say no to the heart fund, the cancer drive, the leukemia foundation and so forth? Usually we cannot.

The problem is that most of us have limited funds. Out of these limited funds we must support our local church, Christian ministries and missions. It's impossible to stretch your dollars to cover everything. Critical choices have to be made. You may indeed be touched by the need represented by the telephone solicitor and will feel led to contribute, but never make a hasty promise. It could turn out to be a lie. Instead, tell the caller to send you some information about that charity. Tell him you have to weigh your obligations. And then pray about it. Give yourself some time to get some guidance from God for even these routine matters of life. Don't compromise God's resources by making hasty promises. Know what His priorities are and then follow them.

Hasty commitments

Time is another precious commodity that can be compromised by haste. The temptation to overcommit ourselves is universal. We see so many needs: the Sunday school needs teachers, the youth need sponsors, the church needs deacons, the mission needs volunteers. Before you know it, you have promised to do it all. "I'll pray the Lord gives me strength," you say. Sometimes you learn the hard way that God gives strength for what He wants you to do— but not for the 101 other things you feel you need to do.

You cannot meet every need, and you are not called to meet every need. If you have no time for your family, if you have difficulty finding time to get alone with God, if your health is faltering because you are so exhausted meeting your commitments, likely you've said yes more often than God led you to.

When someone requests for more of your time, don't commit immediately. Again, tell him you need an opportunity to pray for God's green light. Rarely should you make a commitment on the spot. Get away from the woeful eyes and pleading voice and listen to God instead. Talk it over with your spouse and pray together (he or she is the one who usually suffers the most when you are overextended). Then, when you reach a decision, stick to it.

Hasty conclusions

In addition, never come to a hasty conclusion. Like one office worker said to another, "We don't need a fitness program. People around here get plenty of exercise jumping to conclusions." Hasty conclusions are often based only on partial facts, and the consequences can be embarrassing.

The Piltdown Man, discovered in 1912 near Piltdown, England, was supposedly proof of the ape-like character of early man. This conclusion was based on some fragments of a skull and a jawbone. More than 500 doctoral theses were written on this subject. In 1953, however, it was discovered that the bones had been gathered together and placed in a shallow grave by a practical joker. They didn't even come from the same carcass. Hundreds of scholars had been embarrassed by jumping to the wrong conclusion. "Do you see a man hasty in his words? There is more hope for a fool than for him."

Hasty retorts

Have you noticed that the first words that come to mind are often not our best words? When these words are inspired by anger or sarcasm, they can be devastating. British author and playwright George Bernard Shaw once sent Sir Winston Churchill two tickets to the opening night's performance of one of his plays. Accompanying the tickets was Shaw's short note, "Bring a friend, if you have one." Churchill, also adept at saying a lot in a few words, replied: "I'll wait for the second night, if there is one." Such cuts and jabs may not be fatal but they are painful. They are wounds we should not inflict upon either friend or foe. "A fool vents all his feelings, but a wise man holds them back" (Prov. 29:11).

A mouth opened in haste to make a promise, to incur a commitment, to draw a conclusion or to speak a word in retort can become a reason for regret that lasts a long time. Instead, we need to follow the wisdom in Proverbs 13:3: "He who guards his mouth preserves his life, but he who opens wide his lips shall have destruction" (13:3).

Lying words

Clubhouse Magazine, published by Focus on the Family, conducted a contest in which kids were asked to give the best excuse they had ever given for not doing their homework. One boy wrote, "I went on a hot air balloon ride and we were going to crash because there was too much weight in the basket, so I threw my homework out and it saved our lives." Where do kids get this kind of "creativity"? Likely from their parents.

"Mommy, what is a lie?" a little boy asked. His mother answered, "Son, a lie is an abomination unto the Lord—but a very present help in time of need!" By our attitudes and actions, we often teach our children just how true this is.

Writing in *Boardroom Reports*, Peter LeVine revealed, "When the Port Authority of New York and New Jersey ran a help-wanted ad for electricians with expertise at using Sontag connectors, it got 170 responses even though there is no such thing as a Sontag connector. The Authority ran the ad to find out how many applicants falsify resumes."

Of the seven things that are an abomination to the Lord, recorded in Proverbs 6:16–19, "a false witness who speaks lies" is one of the most damaging. We lie much more often than we realize. One survey showed 91 percent of Americans lie routinely. Perhaps we don't even recognize some ways in which we lie. But Scripture says we are lying when we:

Leave out the truth

This is the first lie in the Bible, told by the Father of Lies himself. In Genesis 3:1, Satan asked Eve, "Has God indeed said, 'You shall not eat of every tree of the garden'?" This seems like an innocent question, but behind it are several unspoken lies. First, Satan knew what God had really said. As the Prince of the Air with a host of demons at his command, it is likely that he knew of any conversation God had with Adam and Eve. Second, Satan was implying that God would be so strict that He would forbid them to eat from "every tree of the garden." By withholding the truth that God had Adam's and Eve's best interest at heart, Satan lied.

When you imply something false by withholding the whole truth, you lie. Allowing someone else to take the blame when you are at fault is a lie. Failing to speak out with the truth when someone else is propagating error is a lie. Silence is not always golden; sometimes it's a plain lie.

Add to the truth

In response to Satan, Eve also lied. She said, "We may eat the fruit of the trees of the garden; but of the fruit of the tree which is in the midst of the garden, God has said, 'You shall not eat it, *nor shall you touch it*, lest you die'" (Gen. 3:2–3, italics mine). God had said nothing about touching the fruit (Gen. 2:17). By adding to what God had said, Eve told a lie. "Do not add to His words," Proverbs 30:6 warns, "lest He reprove you, and you be found a liar."

When we repeat what others say, we stand a good chance of telling a lie even if we don't mean to. Somehow the truth loses its accuracy the more mouths and ears it has to pass through. Do you remember playing the "telephone game" when you were a child? You passed a message down the line by whispering it in the next person's ear. Invariably, by the time it reached the end of the line, the message was so radically changed it was unrecognizable.

When you must repeat something verbally (such as a prayer request), check to make sure you have all the facts straight. Don't intermingle your interpretation of the facts with the facts themselves and thus "enhance" the truth. Adding to the truth is just as much a lie as not telling the whole truth.

Contradict the truth

The Garden of Eden story also includes blatant lies. Satan said, "You will not surely die. For God knows that in the day you eat of it your eyes will be opened, and you will be like God, knowing good and evil" (Gen. 3:4-5). That is a direct contradiction of what God said (see Gen. 2:16–17). God is truth; therefore, whenever we contradict Him, we are lying.

A group of Protestant and Catholic academicians are touring the United States with a presentation called the "Jesus Seminar." It is an obvious attempt to contradict God. These so-called theologians assert that, among other things, Mary was not a virgin when she bore Jesus, He did not descend from King David, He was not born in Bethlehem, there was no slaughter of the infants, and Christ's birth did not take place at the time of the census described in Luke. When we deny the Word, we find ourselves caught in a liar's web— and we even begin believing the lies we tell others.

God's wisdom warns us about lies. Whatever their shape and form, big or little, untruths must be avoided. Proverbs 17:4 says, "An evildoer gives heed to false lips; a liar listens eagerly to a spiteful tongue."

God's guide for life's choices also tells us of other kinds of words that should be avoided by all who want to please Him.

Hurtful words

When you were a child, did you ever chant, "Sticks and stones may break my bones but words will never hurt me?" Now that you are older, you realize just how untrue that childish ditty is. Words can be very hurtful. They are especially hurtful if they are:

Bloody words

These are words that incite bloodshed. They are fighting words, sinister words, words filled with venom. "The words of the wicked are, 'Lie in wait for blood'" (Prov. 12:6a).

In November 1995 the world was shocked at the assassination of Israeli Prime Minister Yitzhak Rabin. He was slain by a 25-year-old student who claimed, "I acted alone on

God's orders, and I have no regrets." But the months leading up to this crime had been filled with words of hate poured out upon the prime minister. Leaders of the Jewish settler movement had branded him a traitor for negotiating the return of land to the Palestinians. Extremist rabbis called him a murderer and said it would be morally acceptable to kill him.[1]

We Christians are not entirely innocent in using such words. The more conservative branches of the Church not only have fought for fundamental principles of the faith, some also have fought among themselves over issues that are far from fundamental. The singing of praise choruses versus traditional hymns, the use of tile or carpet for the fellowship hall and other equally unimportant matters have been fuel for the flames. George Sweeting wrote, "Contentious tongues have hindered the work of God a thousand times over. Critical tongues have closed church doors. Careless tongues have broken the hearts and health of many pastors. The sins of the tongue have besmirched the pure white garments of the bride of Christ."[2] Let's commit that, by God's grace, such hurtful words will never pass from our lips.

Gossiping words

In Alice Roosevelt Longworth's sitting room was a pillow with the embroidered motto, "If you can't say anything good about someone, sit right here by me." Unfortunately, many people are willing to accept the invitation. The hurt that results from gossip is tragic. Proverbs 17:9 warns, "He who repeats a matter separates the best of friends."

Someone personified gossip and said, "I tear down homes, break hearts, wreck lives. I travel on the wings of the wind. No innocence is strong enough to intimidate me, no purity pure enough to daunt me. I have no regard for truth, no respect for justice, no mercy for the defenseless."

God's wisdom says, "The words of a talebearer are like tasty trifles, and they go down into the inmost body" (Prov.

18:8). The Hebrew word for "tasty trifles" literally means "things greedily devoured." In our hearts, most of us enjoy a juicy bit of gossip. But hearing gossip is like eating something delicious that, once ingested, never seems to set right in your stomach. Gossip is destructive to the gossiper as well as to the one gossiped about. Even though most people like to hear gossip, they do not respect the one gossiping. It tarnishes our testimony and turns us into birds of prey, always looking for the next morsel. "A talebearer reveals secrets, but he who is of a faithful spirit conceals a matter" (Prov. 11:13).

How can we avoid gossip? Alan Redpath offered this solution. Before speaking of any person or subject, ask yourself:

T — Is it true?

H — Is it helpful?

I — Is it inspiring?

N — Is it necessary?

K — Is it kind? [3]

Think. If we were to think of the harm gossip does both to us and others, if we were to follow this simple formula, imagine how much hurtful gossip would be eliminated.

Harsh words

Although harsh words are frequently used in the heat of the moment, they are never the answer to a problem. Instead, Proverbs 15:1 says, "A soft answer turns away wrath, but a harsh word stirs up anger." In other words, a gentle answer can defuse a potentially explosive situation, but a harsh answer worsens the situation.

Researchers from the Speech Research Unit at Kenyon College in Ohio discovered that people addressed by the telephone or intercom respond in the same tone of voice that they hear. Even when they consciously try to answer in an opposite tone— a quiet voice to a loud one, or a gentle voice to an angry one— they have a hard time doing so. [4]

This is important to know both in the home and the workplace. If as a parent you use angry, harsh words that hit your children like blows from a sledgehammer, you may find yourself living for a lifetime with a crushed son or daughter. Words that explode at an impressionable moment can rarely be forgotten.

One pastor told of a 42-year-old man named Tom. As one who frantically worked himself into exhaustion, Tom spent every dime he made for impressive artifacts of luxury and success. He had a volatile temper that exploded at the slightest hint of disagreement or criticism. The pastor asked Tom to tell him about his childhood.

At one impressionable point in his boyhood, Tom said, he displeased his father with the way he did a chore. His father said, "Tom, you'll always be a bum!" Whenever he and his father had angry moments, his father made the same prediction, so that eventually it burrowed its way into Tom's spirit like shrapnel embedded in flesh. Thirty years later, he still suffered from his father's verbal abuse. Even though his father was dead, Tom remained unsure whether or not his father's prediction had come true. When anyone suggested that Tom was doing something wrong, he unleashed a barrage of hostility because of old accusations from his thoughtless father.

Be very careful of the words you say to your children, especially in anger. Harsh words can create wounds that last a lifetime, but a "gentle answer turns away wrath."

The other side of the coin

Thankfully, what passes from our lips always is not always hurtful and harmful. The wisdom of God says, "Death *and* life are in the power of the tongue" (Prov. 18:21, italics mine). Both can be found in our use of words. The destructive side of the tongue, as we have seen, is reflected in hasty, lying, hurtful words. These can destroy those around us spiritually, emotionally and physically. But there is a beneficial side to words. It is seen when we use words in a positive way.

God's wisdom has as much to say about the proper use of words as it has to say about the misuse of words. The vocabulary of helpful words includes:

Inspiring words

Proverbs says, "Pleasant words are like a honeycomb, sweetness to the soul and health to the bones" (Prov. 16:24). The English word *pleasant* is derived from a Hebrew word that means "delightful, inspiring or uplifting." Inspiring words help a person feel better. They are always pleasant and delightful.

Comforting words

According to Webster's Dictionary, *comfort* is composed of two Latin words— *com*, meaning "with," and *forte*, meaning "strength." So the word *comfort* literally means "with strength."

Sometimes it's difficult to say the right words to a friend. We don't always know how to comfort someone and give him the strength to go on when he has experienced a significant loss. Who better to tell us than someone who has lost the dearest person in life? One widow suggests the following responses:

"What I always liked about _____ was _____."

"I'll never forget the time he and I _____ ."

"It's OK. Tell me again about _____."

"I just phoned to say hello."

"Tuesday will be a tough day for you. May we spend it together?"

"I thought you might need a hug or someone to hold your hand today."

"I'd love to (trim bushes, etc.). May I do it for you?"

This widow summarized by saying the best thing anybody who did not know her husband personally ever said to her was, "I was so sorry to read about your husband's death. Would you like to talk about it?"[5]

Everyone suffers. When we experience a loss, grief is inevitable. We need never grieve alone, however, if our friends are tuned in to God's wisdom and have learned to bring words of comfort to strengthen us during difficult times.

The sequoia trees of California tower as much as 300 feet above the ground. Oddly, these enormous trees have unusually shallow roots that reach out in all directions to capture the greatest amount of surface moisture. Seldom do redwoods stand alone because high winds would quickly uproot them. Instead they grow in clusters. Their intertwining roots provide strength for one another against the storms.

If you need the strength of others today, allow the roots of your life to intertwine with theirs. And be alert for opportunities to lend strength to others who are suffering. There is nothing quite like words of comfort when we need them most.

Encouraging words

A Japanese proverb says, "One kind word can warm three winter months." In a cold, impersonal world, how desperately we need to be inspired by the warm words of encouragement.

Not far from Lincoln, Nebraska, is a wildlife refuge that is filled every fall with thousands of migrating Canadian geese. These large birds, who fly great distances across continents, have three remarkable qualities. First, since breaking the wind barrier is a tough job for the lead goose, they rotate leadership. No one bird stays out in front all the time. Second, they fly in a V formation because that requires 71 percent less energy for each bird compared with flying solo. Third, during the entire time one bird is leading, the rest are honking their affirmation.

Christians need to follow the example of the Canadian geese and express our encouragement to one another. In their book *The Blessing*, Gary Smalley and John Trent observe that "the family blessing hinges on being a spoken message. Abraham spoke a blessing to Isaac. Isaac spoke it to his son Jacob. Jacob spoke it to each of his twelve sons and to two of his grandchildren. Esau was so excited when he was called in to receive his blessing because, after years of waiting, he would finally hear the blessing. In the Scriptures, a blessing is not a blessing unless it is spoken."[6] The encouragement we receive even from a small amount of affirmation can keep us going through the hard times, if someone just remembers to say it.

When was the last time you made a special effort to tell someone, "You did a great job!" "I believe you can do it!" "I'm so glad you're my wife (husband, son, daughter)." Your spouse, children or friends are not mind readers. All your good thoughts and good intentions are worthless unless you speak them. "My son, if your heart is wise, my heart will rejoice— indeed, I myself; yes, my inmost being will rejoice when your lips speak right things" (Prov. 23:15–16).

Instructive words

One of the finest qualities of the Proverbs 31 woman is her ability to instruct with words of wisdom. Verse 26 says, "She opens her mouth with wisdom, and on her tongue is the law of kindness." Tragically, people today would rather be entertained than edified. They want to be titillated rather than taught. But for those with ears to hear and hearts open to receive, words of instruction can change their lives.

God's wisdom is not theoretical; it is practical. Add the power of the Holy Spirit to words faithfully spoken, and who can walk away unchanged? Wisdom says, "A wise man will hear and increase learning, and a man of understanding will attain wise counsel" (Prov. 1:5). Whatever our age or status, we all need words of instruction. It is important that we teach:

Our children

Many parents today are making a critical mistake in raising their children. They leave the academic training up to the school system and the spiritual training up to the church. Frankly, both are inadequate for the job. When a teacher has to divide her attention between 20–30 children in a classroom and Sunday school lasts only one hour a week, how is it possible for our children to learn all they need to be taught? It is still the parents' responsibility to oversee the education of their children.

Typically, parents say, "I don't have time." It does take a lot of time and energy to be involved in your child's intellectual and spiritual growth, but surely you have more time than Susannah Wesley had. Mrs. Wesley lived before the day of automatic washers and driers or disposable diapers. She had 19 children. In spite of what must have been a hectic schedule, she spent one hour each day praying for her children. In addition, she took each child aside for a full hour every week to discuss spiritual matters. No wonder two of her sons, Charles and John, were used of God to bring blessing to the world.

Susannah Wesley followed a few simple rules in training her children:

1. Subdue self-will in a child and thus work together with God to save his soul.

2. Teach him to pray as soon as he can speak.

3. Give him nothing he cries for and only what is good for him if he asks for it politely.

4. To prevent lying, punish no fault that is freely confessed, but never allow a rebellious, sinful act to go unnoticed.

5. Commend and reward good behavior.

6. Strictly observe all promises you have made to your child.

These rules reflect a combination of tough motherhood and common sense. They establish parameters, recognize the value of prevention and reward performance. Many parents could calm a gathering storm if they followed Mrs. Wesley's advice from God's guidebook.

Our peers

Great musicians never stop taking steps to improve. The well-known concert pianist Arthur Rubinstein used to say that if he missed a day of practice, he noticed it in the quality of his performance. If he missed two days, his critics noticed. And if he missed three days, the audience noticed. No one is so talented or knowledgeable that he can afford to stop learning.

The wisdom of Proverbs reminds us, "As iron sharpens iron, so a man sharpens the countenance of his friend" (Prov. 27:17). Every Christian would profit from being in a teaching or discipling relationship.

Legendary UCLA basketball coach John Wooden taught basketball according to the simplest pedagogical principles. He followed four laws of learning: explanation, demonstration, correction and repetition. When UCLA built the Pauley Pavilion in 1965, Wooden made sure he did not get just an arena but a classroom with bleachers that roll back.[7] He knew he had to do more than just coach his players; he had to teach them as well.

As they grow older, some Christians lose their teachability. They become frozen in their view of Scripture and adopt the motto, "As it was in the beginning, is now, and ever shall be." Sadly, they lose the joy of encountering the Living Word in a fresh way and the blessing of being ministered to by the insights of others.

Whether it's in a Sunday school class, an adult Bible study or a one-on-one discipling relationship, don't miss out on being sharpened by your peers. Study the Word so you can sharpen others as well. Saint Jerome said, "The Bible is shallow enough for a lamb to wade in it yet deep enough for an elephant to swim in it." We never outgrow our need to teach and be taught the Scriptures.

Timely words

It is just as important to speak at the right time as it is to speak the right words. God is a master in the art of timeliness. Romans 5:6 says, "For when we were still without strength, in due time [i.e., at the right time] Christ died for the ungodly." Elsewhere Paul wrote, "But when the fullness of the time had come, God sent forth His Son, born of a woman, born under the law, to redeem those who were under the law, . . . that we might receive the adoption as sons" (Gal. 4:4–5). God speaks through His actions, and He always acts at just the right time.

We should cultivate godlikeness in this area. We, too, need to speak at the right time. God's wisdom says, "A word fitly spoken is like apples of gold in settings of silver" (Prov. 25:11). When our timing is right, our words become:

Relevant

The old adage says, "It's too late to lock the barn door after the horse is stolen." In other words, locking the door is no longer relevant. When we speak either words of warning or words of comfort, we need to make sure that what we have to say is relevant. Timing is the key.

In the early days of the Dallas Cowboys football team, things didn't go so well. They lost game after game and most people blamed Coach Tom Landry. His critics accused him of not having enthusiasm and not pumping up his players for each game. On one particular day the sportswriters were amazed to see the Cowboys come roaring out of the locker room and race across the field. When the reporters caught up with Landry they asked, "What did you say to get the players so charged up?" Landry replied, "Oh, it was easy. I simply said, 'The last eleven guys to the bench have to start.'"

When our timing is right, our words gain new power. They are no longer just good advice; they are words that change lives.

Acceptable

Communication is much more than speaking. It is speaking, hearing and responding. Not only must we speak, but the words we say must be accepted by the one who is listening. What's more, a response must follow. Some words—such as the salvation message—are always relevant. There is never a time when an unsaved person doesn't need to hear about Christ's saving power. But there are times when people are more open to hear and respond than at others.

When a disobedient boy became a young man, he left home, scoffing at his mother's prayers that he would turn to Christ. He went off to sea without even saying good-bye to her. On his first voyage the ship lurched and he was thrown overboard. Quickly, a lifeboat was lowered and he was rescued just as he was slipping beneath the water's surface, never to rise again. Everyone thought he was dead, but the ship's doctor revived him. When he opened his eyes, his first words were, "Jesus has saved my soul!" After he was completely recovered, he told how, in that awful moment, he remembered a text his mother had taught him years before: "This is a faithful saying, and worthy of all acceptance, that Christ Jesus came into the world to save sinners, of whom I am chief" (1 Tim. 1:15). He said, "As I was sinking, I cast myself into the outstretched arms of the Savior."

Are you praying for a son or daughter who is far from the Lord today? Should you quit? Not a chance. Our prayers for wayward children, coupled with acceptable words of warning and encouragement, are never forgotten. No wonder the Bible says, "A man has joy by the answer of his mouth, and a word spoken in due season, how good it is!" (Prov. 15:23).

Words, words . . . and more words

Do we talk too much? Frequently we do. The average person spends one-fifth of his or her life talking. If all of our words were put into print, a single day's worth would fill a 50-page book. In a year's time we would fill more than 90 books of 200 pages each. With such a productive output, isn't it important that we govern our words by God's wisdom? Here is some sage counsel from Proverbs regarding too many words.

Proverbs 10:19 says, "In the multitude of words sin is not lacking, but he who restrains his lips is wise." Constant talking will inevitably lead to sin. "Whoever guards his mouth and tongue keeps his soul from troubles" (Prov. 21:23). Perhaps we adults should sing that children's chorus more often: "Oh, be careful little tongue what you say. . . ."

When we talk too much we betray ourselves. The quickest way to give the impression of wisdom is to say nothing. Abraham Lincoln said it this way: "It is better to be quiet and be thought a fool, than to open your mouth and remove all doubt." Or, as Solomon said, "He who has knowledge spares his words . . . Even a fool is counted wise when he holds his peace" (Prov. 17:27–28). Sometimes we forget that we need to listen twice as much as we talk. Not only will we learn more, but we will be perceived as being wise enough not to speak when we have nothing to say.

We need to pray each day:

Lord, grant this one request I pray:
Guide thou my tongue!

The words I say can never be called back again,
should they cause anger, sorrow, pain
then in an ever-widening sphere,
they spread their havoc far and near.
So guide my tongue in every word,
that it may bless where'er it's heard.

— Anonymous

Choose your words carefully. Fortunately, we have a handbook that helps us select just the right word, the word that will lift others up instead of pushing them down. That handbook is Proverbs, God's guide for right choices. Remember, "death and life are in the power of the tongue." Such power requires careful thought and much caution.

---

[1] Anthony Lewis, "Once again we learn that words of hate have consequences," *Lincoln Journal Star*, November 7, 1995, p. 6A.

[2] George Sweeting, *How to Solve Conflicts* (Chicago: Moody Press, 1973), pp. 77-78.

[3] David L. Olford, ed., *A Passion for Preaching* (Nashville, Tenn.: Thomas Nelson, 1989), pp. 159-160.

[4] Research of the Speech Research Unit, Kenyon College, Gambier, Ohio, as quoted in *Boardroom Reports*, April 1, 1995, p. 7.

[5] "Dear Abby," *Lincoln Journal Star*, October 8, 1994.

[6] Gary Smalley & John Trent, *The Blessing* (Nashville, Tenn.: Thomas Nelson, 1982), p. 49.

[7] *Sports Illustrated*, April 3, 1989, p. 100.

Chapter 12

Wisdom and
Your Faith

*Trust in the LORD with all your heart, and lean not on your
own understanding; in all your ways acknowledge Him,
and He shall direct your paths.*
Proverbs 3:5-6

Perhaps the hardest time to use God's Word to guide your actions is when you need to use it the most—when disaster strikes. Our initial response is usually, "Why? Why me? Why now?" Often there are no answers to these questions. God is silent and our cries go unanswered. This is when we have to rely on faith.

Some years ago I knew a pastor who served in a church just north of the city where I lived. Leaving a Tuesday evening church committee meeting, he was tragically killed when another car plowed into him shortly after he pulled onto the highway in front of the church. The pastor was rushed to the hospital, but to no avail. The church lost a beloved leader.

The next morning I called some of the elders to express my sympathies and offered to fill the pulpit on Sunday if they had a need. They were grateful and immediately said, "Oh, please do that." After I hung up I realized that their next service would be that night, not Sunday. I called again and asked if they needed someone for their Wednesday evening service. Again they expressed thanks.

That evening I stood before a heartbroken congregation. Stunned grievers throughout the sanctuary wept. As I realized the depth of their sorrow, Proverbs 3:5-6 came to my mind, so I shared that with them: "Trust in the LORD with all your heart, and lean not on your own understanding; in all your ways acknowledge Him, and He shall direct your paths." In the midst of disaster, those verses comforted that congregation and renewed their hope.

Of course, not all of life's disasters involve death. It may be your teenage daughter has caved in to social pressure and now is pregnant. It may be your biopsy is back from the lab and your doctor wants to see you. Perhaps one of your spiritual heroes has fallen into sin, or your husband tells you he doesn't love you anymore, or your house burns down and you lose everything. Disaster strikes in many ways. Regardless of what form it takes, there is more to handling a disaster than asking why it happened. God's wisdom says we should look to faith in the dark days of disaster. Proverbs 3:5-6 outlines three steps and a promise that, if we are willing to use them, will guide us through the tough times of life.

Step 1: Trust in the Lord

The word *trust* in Hebrew is *batach* (baw-takh). It means literally "to take refuge" or "to find security." Old Testament scholar G. R. Driver says that the word originally had the idea of lying helplessly face down. It's one thing to lie on your back and watch the clouds go by. From that position you can quickly leap to your feet at the first sign of trouble. But to be on your face with your nose pressed into the dirt and your hands stretched out ahead of you leaves you vulnerable. You would lie face down only if you felt a sense of safety and trust.

Others have suggested that *trust* is a wrestling term and is the equivalent of a body slam. When an opponent is hoisted into the air and then slammed to the canvas, he usually does not get up right away. He is stunned, breathless and helpless.

When you face a personal or family disaster, you do not causally bump into Jehovah. Instead, you are body slammed at His feet. You have no choices, no alternate plans. You are helplessly dependent on God, which is where He wants us and where we need to be.

Depending on God is easier said than done because Americans in particular are raised with an admiration for people who are self-reliant. To lie helplessly before God, to totally rest ourselves in Him, is contrary to our culture. It feels unnatural, even wrong, to put ourselves in such a position. Yet this is what trust demands of us.

Trust that God is in control

Is God really in control? Some people argue that if a good God is in control, there shouldn't be so much evil in the world. As they view it, the presence of evil means either that God is not good or that He is not in control.

Scripture affirms that God is good. "The goodness of God endures continually" (Ps. 52:1). "Oh, give thanks to the LORD, for He is good!" (1 Chron. 16:34). "Praise the LORD! Oh, give thanks to the LORD, for He is good!" (Ps. 106:1). If God is good, does this mean He is not in control?

No, God is in control, but we have to understand where disaster comes from. Things that break our hearts and threaten to destroy the fabric of our lives are not the products of God but the consequences of sin. God's Word says, "Therefore, just as through one man sin entered the world, and death through sin, and thus death spread to all men, because all sinned" (Rom. 5:12). Sin brought death into the world, and with it came all the other evils we experience.

To rid the world of all sin would take a drastic measure. Since sin is part of man's nature, the only way God could remove it would be to eliminate man. But as long as people are responding to the Gospel message, God withholds His final judgment (Matt. 24:14).

In the meantime, God does not put His people in plastic bubbles to protect us from the effects of sin. He does not always prevent the consequences of living in a sin-filled world from touching those of us who belong to Him. But He does give us this promise: "And we know that all things work together for good to those who love God, to those who are the called according to His purpose" (Rom. 8:28). That's not just a crutch; it is the affirmation of a good God.

Because God is in control, He is able to take the disasters that invade our lives and cause them to work for our good. That doesn't make evil good. Sin is ugly any way you view it. But we need not despair. Nothing can happen to a child of God that cannot be turned to our benefit through the power of the loving, omnipotent God.

Trust in God's wisdom

A mountain climber was scaling a steep cliff when his foot slipped and he started to fall. As he waved his hands to keep his balance, he brushed against a sturdy bush growing out of a crevice in the rock. Grabbing hold, he kept himself from falling, but he was stuck. He couldn't get a foothold to go either forward or backward. All he could do was hang on. He began to cry for help. "I can help you," a voice from above him said, "but you've got to let go of the bush." The climber thought for a moment and then called out, "Is there anyone else who can help me?"

When God speaks in the midst of a crisis, we are sometimes like that climber. We hear what He says, but it's so hard to trust His solutions. We ask ourselves, *How can that possibly help?* or, *How do I know I can trust God?*

Sometimes we don't want to accept God's solutions. They seem too hard. They involve things like forgiving our enemies (Matt. 5:43-44), letting go of our bitterness (Eph. 4:31; Heb. 12:15) or thanking Him for our problems (Phil. 4:6).

God's wisdom doesn't always seem like the logical path to follow. But that's all the more reason to do things His way. In Isaiah 55:8–9 God says, "'For My thoughts are not your thoughts, nor are your ways My ways,' says the Lord. 'For as the heavens are higher than the earth, so are My ways higher than your ways, and My thoughts than your thoughts.'" It is not your responsibility to judge the logic of God's ways; you are simply to trust Him. As Job said, "Though He slay me, yet will I trust Him" (Job 13:15).

Trust with a whole heart

Furthermore, the wisdom of God's Word calls us to trust "with all our heart" (Prov. 3:5). We cannot trust God in every area of our lives except two or three. It won't even work to trust with 99 percent of our heart. God wants the whole. If a wife were faithful to her husband 99 percent of the time, we would still call her unfaithful. Likewise, God will settle for nothing less than a trust that fills our heart.

John Paton was a missionary to the New Hebrides islands (now Vanuatu) in the South Seas. While translating the Bible for one of the tribes, he discovered that they had no word for *trust* or *faith.* One day a native who had been running hard came into the missionary's house. With complete abandonment, the man flopped himself in a large chair and said, "It is good to rest my whole weight on this chair." It never crossed his mind to wonder if the chair would hold him. "That's it!" Paton exclaimed. "I'll translate *faith* and *trust* as 'resting one's whole weight on God.'"

Trusting God means that we give ourselves wholly to Him. We let our complete weight rest on Him. Such an attitude is foreign to us. We have a hard time doing that, yet when there's nothing else left, it always works. As the words of a popular song say, "When you can't trace His hand, trust His heart."

Step 2: Lean not on your own understanding

The word for *understanding* in Hebrew communicates the idea of trying to figure something out. It comes from a root word meaning "to separate mentally," that is, to try to break it down into pieces and figure out how all the parts fit together.

God's wisdom warns us not to trust or place our weight on our own understanding. Trusting ourselves and our wisdom is the first inclination of humanity and the last refuge of failure. Every time we ask why, we open a file labeled "our own understanding." "Why did my tax forms get audited?" "Why did God allow my husband to die?" "Why did our church go through a split?" Whenever we get into this frame of mind, we end up spinning our wheels. Often there are no answers to these questions and we only get frustrated. We need to realize the truth about our understanding.

It is faulty

When Intel® introduced the first Pentium® chips (the "brains" that operate many personal computers), it was discovered they were flawed. When some researchers needed to carry a decimal place to the far right, there was a potential error.

This error affected only a small percentage of users, yet a general outcry was heard from Pentium® owners. Whether they used that feature or not, in their eyes the chip was flawed and should be replaced.

Yet history has shown over and over again that our ability to reason is far more flawed than the Pentium® chip. For example, Lord Kelvin, British mathematician, physicist and president of the British Royal Society, in 1895 pronounced, "Heavier-than-air flying machines are impossible." (The Wright brothers flew their first airplane on December 17, 1903.) In August 1968 Business Week stated, "With over fifty foreign cars already on sale here, the Japanese auto industry isn't likely to carve out a big slice of the U.S. market for itself." (In 1980 Japan had 2.1 million sales in the United States, beating out every domestic car manufacturer.)

Other blemishes in our understanding are even more embarrassing. "A severe depression like that of 1920-1921 is outside the range of probability," said the Harvard Economic Society on November 16, 1929. (The stock market crash of October 29, 1929, sent the U.S. economy into the worst depression on record, lasting until the beginning of World War II.) "No matter what happens, the U.S. Navy is not going to be caught napping," assured Frank Knox,

Secretary of the Navy, on December 4, 1941, just three days before the Japanese attack on Pearl Harbor.

When we lean on our own understanding, we're trusting ourselves to very flawed thinking. If our own wisdom is so faulty that we cannot come to appropriate temporal conclusions, how can we trust our understanding for eternal decisions?

It is inadequate

Not only do we often get the facts wrong, we usually don't possess all the facts to begin with— certainly not enough to come to a sound and error-free conclusion. What we need is someone who knows everything. Admittedly, there are a few people around who think they do. Columnist Ann Landers reported the following ad in a local paper: "For sale: Complete set of Encyclopedia Britannica. Never used. My husband knows everything." Even the experts have difficulty keeping up with the latest developments in their area.

But there is One who does know all the facts. The psalmist says to God, "You know my sitting down and my rising up; you understand my thought afar off. You comprehend my path and my lying down, and are acquainted with all my ways" (Ps. 139:2-3). God truly does know it all and He forgets nothing except what He chooses not to hold against us (Heb. 8:12).

Yet it takes more than the facts to reach a right understanding. For a complete, fault-free judgment, it's not enough to know what has happened; we also need to know why. We need to understand the motive that lies behind the action or event.

Again, this knowledge is beyond our reach as humans. When Jesus commanded, "Judge not, that you be not judged" (Matt. 7:1), it was this type of judgment He was talking about. Obviously we are called to inspect other people's actions— how else can we rebuke, exhort or commend (see 1 Tim. 6:2; 2 Tim 4:2)? But when we pass judgment on people's motives, we've gone beyond our understanding and into a realm only God is able to know.

Without all the facts, it is best to trust God's understanding rather than our own. The words of Woodrow Wilson, the 28th president of the United States, still ring true: "There are a good many problems before the American people today, and before me as president, but I expect to find the solution of those problems just in the proportion that I am faithful in the study of the Word of God." As we trust God's wisdom instead of our own, He will provide a way.

Step 3: In all your ways acknowledge Him

When we acknowledge someone we recognize his presence. When a friend comes into the room and you acknowledge him, it means you are aware who he is and that he is present with you. God's wisdom says that we should see His presence in every area of our lives ("in all your ways"). However, it is easy to forget that God is always present because we cannot see Him.

One Christmas Eve the telephone rang in the office of a pastor in Washington, D.C. The man pastored the church that President Franklin Roosevelt attended. "Tell me, Reverend," the voice inquired, "are you holding a Christmas Eve service tonight?" When the pastored indicated they were, the caller asked, "And do you expect President Roosevelt to attend your church tonight?" "That I can't promise," explained the pastor. "I'm not sure about the president's plans for this evening. But I can say that we fully expect God to be in our church tonight." The president may not always be in attendance, but God is.

To remind us of God's presence, David and Karen Mains have a game they recommend to all Christians. It's called the "I Spy" game. They used it around the supper table when their children were growing up. Each person was asked where he "spied" God during his day. It might be that he saw God provide a parking place close to where he needed to go, or perhaps God permitted a flat tire just as he was pulling into a filling station.

God is not a stranger to us. Every day, in so many different ways, He manifests His presence in our lives. We fail to recognize His presence when we fail to see our world through the eyes of faith. We need to cultivate the spiritual sight necessary to spy God. When we learn to recognize Him, we may be surprised at how frequently He intervenes in the daily affairs of our life.

It keeps us from sin

Living with the realization that Christ is constantly with us becomes a strong motivation to avoid sin. There are places we will not go simply because we would be ashamed to take Christ with us. There are words we will not speak because we do not want Jesus to hear such things coming out of our mouth.

When tempted to sin, visualize Christ's presence in your life. Picture Him beside you. Feel the hurt that He would feel if you carried out your plans. This should be a strong deterrent to the sins we otherwise would fall prey to. Then rejoice with the writer of "How Firm a Foundation," who reminds of God's promise, "Fear not, I am with thee— O be not dismayed, For I am thy God, I will still give thee aid; I'll strengthen thee, help thee and cause thee to stand, Upheld by my gracious, omnipotent hand."

The knowledge that God is with us in the Person of the Holy Spirit everywhere we go, that He is aware of every word we say and that He is privy to every thought we think, should be a strong deterrent to sinful living. It is only when our consciences becomes seared, desensitized to our sin, that we are no longer concerned with God's abiding presence.

It keeps us from quitting

Missionary and explorer David Livingstone voluntarily suffered some of the greatest hardships that men have been called to endure. When he was back in Scotland on furlough from Africa, a student at Glasgow University asked him, "How did you do it? How did you stand the loneliness and hardships?" Livingstone replied, "Because God has said, 'Lo, I am with you always, even to the end of the world.'" Knowing that we are not alone in our difficulties is often the needed inspiration to keep us from throwing in the towel.

When I was a student at the University of Strasbourg in 1970, I was the only English-speaking student on my floor in a French dormitory. My family was back in the United States, so I spent long hours alone. But something wonderful happened a few weeks into my time in France: I remembered that I was not alone. God was my constant companion. When there was nobody else, there was God. It kept me going during the months I was apart from my family. There's no quitting when you have a companion like God.

It keeps us from despairing

Despair is that black darkness that settles over us when we think that all is lost, or worse, that no one cares. Yet God does care and He proves it by His presence.

Earlier I mentioned John Paton, a pioneer missionary to the New Hebrides. He went to the mission field as a young man with a young bride. When their first child was born, the child died and his wife died soon afterwards. He buried them with his own hands. Because he was among cannibals, he sat over the grave for many days and nights to prevent them from digging up the bodies and eating them. His testimony was that if the Lord Jesus Christ had not made Himself real to him during that time, he would have gone mad.

When disaster strikes your life, that's when you need God the most. In Psalm 23 David said, "Yea, though I walk through the valley of the shadow of death, I will fear no evil; for You are with me; Your rod and Your staff, they comfort me" (v.4). The Hebrew translation for "the valley of the shadow of death" is "the valley of dark shadows." Death is certainly a dark shadow, but the operative word here is *shadow*. God is real, and He casts out the shadows of our life when disaster brings despair. That's when it is especially good to know that God is with you.

Whatever your situation, God walks with you. Turn your eyes on Him and be comforted by His presence. LeRoy Eims wrote, "Self-dependence is folly and rebellion is ruin. But to trust in the Lord is a dynamic, adventuresome, exciting lifestyle. Placing our faith totally in the power, goodness, and wisdom of God is the most sensible thing we can do or are ever likely to do."[1]

I said at the beginning of this chapter that Proverbs 3:5-6 outlines three steps and a promise that, if we are willing to use them, will guide our lives through the tough times. We've seen the three steps; now the promise.

The Promise: He shall direct your paths

This is God's unbreakable promise to you: He will direct your paths. Life is so confusing and complex that this divine promise is more than just precious to us; it is a necessity as well. When things really get tough in life, that's when we need the most supernatural guidance.

On a frigid Christmas night in 1776, George Washington, along with 2,400 men and 18 cannons, were ferried across the freezing Delaware River. The daring offensive took the Hessian mercenaries serving with the British completely by surprise. A British loyalist tried to alert the Hessians, but their drunken commander refused to interrupt a card game to receive the message. More than 100 Hessians were killed or wounded, and nearly 1,000 were taken prisoner. Not a single American life was lost.

Why had Washington and his army left behind the warmth of home and hearth? Washington claimed it was because he felt the guiding hand of God. When we trust the Lord, He directs our paths. This means we have the assurance that:

We will be on the right path

When you face a crisis you may receive all kinds of advice from your friends and family. No matter how sincere they are, however, their advice is still human advice that could set you off on the wrong path.

Jim Reapsome, editor of *Pulse* magazine and a regular contributor on the *Back to the Bible* broadcast, told of an experience he had on a flight to Dallas. Shortly before the door was closed on the plane, a husband and wife rushed aboard. Their assigned seats were already taken, so the flight attendant told them to take any open seat. The plane took off and at 31,000 feet over the Sonoran Desert, the couple discovered why their seats had been taken. They were on the wrong concourse. In their hurry, they had rushed down the wrong runway and ended up on the flight to Dallas instead of the one to Chicago. No one questioned their sincerity, but it didn't change the fact that they were on the wrong plane.

God has assured us that He will always set us on the right path. He promises in Isaiah 30:21, "Your ears shall hear a word behind you, saying, 'This is the way, walk in it,' whenever you turn to the right hand or whenever you turn to the left." God may take us down some cold runways, but if we trust Him and do not attempt to lean on our own understanding, He will always see that the concourses lead to the right plane.

He will deal with the obstacles

Does God promise you there will be no obstacles in your pathway if you trust Him? Not at all. Life is filled with bumps, potholes and unexpected curves. But He does promise there won't be any unscalable bumps, uncrossable potholes or unnegotiable curves. As He told Joshua, "No man shall be able to stand before you all the days of your life; as I was with Moses, so I will be with you. I will not leave you nor forsake you. Be strong and of good courage" (Josh. 1:5-6). The key to our success is our implicit trust in God.

Gladys Aylward, missionary to China more than 50 years ago, was forced to flee when the Japanese invaded Yangcheng. But she could not leave her work behind. With only one assistant, she led more than 100 orphans over the mountain toward Free China. In their book, *The Hidden Price of Greatness*, Ray Besson and Ranelda Mack Hunsicker tell what happened next:

> During Gladys's harrowing journey out of war-torn Yangcheng, . . . she grappled with despair as never before. After passing a sleepless night, she faced the morning with no hope of reaching safety. There were too many obstacles. A 12-year-old girl in the group reminded her of their much-loved story of Moses and the Israelites crossing the Red Sea.
>
> "But I'm not Moses," Gladys cried in desperation.
>
> "Of course you aren't," the girl said, "but Jehovah is still God!"

When Gladys and the orphans made it through, they proved once again that no matter how great the difficulties are, God is still God, and we can trust Him.

We have a choice: we can worry or we can trust. We can fret over all the obstacles in our life, or we can let the Lord take care of the obstacles.

A widow who had successfully raised her large family was being interviewed by a reporter. In addition to 6 children of her own, she had adopted 12 other youngsters, and through it all she had maintained stability and an air of confidence. When asked the secret of her outstanding accomplishment, she answered quite surprisingly: "I managed so well because I'm in a partnership!" "What do you mean?" the reporter inquired. The woman replied, "I mean that many years ago I said, 'Lord, I'll do the work and You do the worrying.' And I haven't had an anxious day since." We all could profit by following the example of this mother. When we commit our burdens to the Lord, we also commit the worrying to Him. That is liberating!

We will arrive safely

God never promises that your trip through life will be smooth and untroubled. Your birth certificate came with no guarantees. But you can be certain that if you allow Him to direct your paths, you will arrive safely at the destination He has prepared for you. Jesus said, "I give them eternal life, and they shall never perish; neither shall anyone snatch them out of My hand. My Father, who has given them to Me, is greater than all; and no one is able to snatch them out of My Father's hand" (John 10:28-29).

There is a monastery in Portugal, perched high on a 3,000-foot cliff, that is accessible only by a terrifying ride in a swaying basket. The basket is pulled with a single rope by several strong men. Once, an American tourist visiting the site became nervous halfway up the cliff when he noticed that the rope was old and frayed. Hoping to calm his fears he asked, "How often do you change the rope?" The monk in charge replied, "Whenever it breaks!"

Discovering halfway up a cliff that you're being held by a frayed rope doesn't make for much security! Unfortunately, many people believe they have no better security in their relationship with God. They wonder, *Can I ever really know for sure that I will arrive safely in heaven?* The answer is yes. When God directs our path, the destination is sure. You have to learn to trust His character rather than your intelligence.

Faith works

Corrie ten Boom once asked a parachutist, "How did you feel when you jumped from an airplane with a parachute on your back for the first time?" He answered, "There was only one thought: *It works, it works.*"[2] That's the way we feel when we have faith in God's care for our lives—we know it works.

Has disaster intruded into your life yet? If not, it's most likely on the way. Perhaps there is a bad medical report in your future, or financial reversals are yet to come, or one of your children is heading down the wrong road. I don't know what the disaster will be, and likely you don't either. But whatever it will be, disaster is on its way.

How will you handle the crisis when it comes? Will you try to figure out why it happened to you? Will you chart your own course for dealing with the calamity? Will you make your choices based on the flawed wisdom of your friends? Or will you allow God's wisdom to guide you? The choice is yours, and so are the consequences. Make sure your choice reflects your faith in the character of God. That's the only way to make the right choice.

---

[1] LeRoy Eims, *Wisdom From Above* (Wheaton, Ill.: Victor Books, 1978), p. 58.

[2] Corrie ten Boom, *Each New Day* (Old Tappan, N.J.: Revell, 1977), p. 193.

Chapter 13

Wisdom and Your Commitment

*Most men will proclaim each his own goodness,
but who can find a faithful man?*
Proverbs 20:6

Many Nebraskans take football very seriously, especially here in Lincoln where the University of Nebraska is located. For some fans, their commitment is so strong that they have already purchased season tickets for many years into the future. In fact, there is a local rumor that Coach Tom Osborne comes out before every game and checks the stadium to see if there are any empty seats. As the story goes, he came out before one game and spotted an empty seat way up near the top of the stadium. When he went up to investigate, he found an elderly lady dressed in black sitting next to the empty seat.

"Do you know whom this seat belongs to?" the coach asked.

"Yes, it's my husband's," the little lady said. "But he died."

"I'm sorry to hear that," the coach replied, "but why didn't you invite a relative to come with you?"

"I couldn't," the lady said. "They're all at the funeral."

Whatever else we might say about this woman, no one can deny that she is the epitome of commitment, at least to that football team.

What is commitment?

We all recognize commitment when we see it. We all desire it when it applies to others. But what is it really?

Commitment is an attitude

The verb *to commit* means to give or to entrust something to someone. Commitment, therefore, implies the willingness to give one's self away. Of all the possessions that an individual might have, the most precious is himself. We are all unique. No one is exactly like you are. Therefore, to give yourself away means you are giving something that no one else can give. Yet this most precious gift is what commitment requires.

Furthermore, having given ourselves away, we must adopt a new attitude toward ourselves. We no longer belong to ourselves exclusively. Commitment says that the person or thing to which we have entrusted ourselves has the right to command us. We belong to him. His desires and wishes now come before our own.

In the 19th century era of missions, missionaries often sent out their supplies packed in a coffin. They knew that 19 out of 20 of them would need the coffin either to be buried in a foreign land or to have their body shipped back home. To them, it didn't make any difference. They were not their own. They had entrusted themselves to a Person and a purpose and no longer were under their own command. Their attitude was, "Lord, I am yours. Do with me as You will."

William Borden had such an attitude. Born into a wealthy home, his father was the founder of the company that still bears his name. After William graduated from high school, his father sent him on a cruise around the world. William was so touched by the spiritual needs of the people he met that he committed his life to serve the Lord Jesus Christ as a missionary. He wrote in his journal:

Say "no" to self, "yes" to Jesus every time. . . . In every man's heart there is a throne and a cross. If Christ is on the throne, self is on the cross; and if self, even a little bit, is on the throne, Jesus is on the cross in that man's heart. . . . Lord, I take my hands off, as far as my life is concerned. I put Thee on the throne of my life. Change, cleanse, use me as Thou shalt choose.

George Atley was another whose attitude reflected commitment. While serving with the Central African Mission, Atley was confronted by a band of hostile tribesmen. He was carrying a fully loaded, ten-chamber Winchester rifle and had to choose either to shoot his attackers and run the risk of negating the work of the mission in that area, or not to defend himself and be killed. When his body was later found in a stream, it was evident that he had chosen the latter. Nearby lay his rifle— all ten chambers still loaded. He had made the supreme sacrifice, motivated by his burden for lost souls and his answering devotion to his Savior. Like the apostle Paul, he wanted Christ to be magnified in his body, "whether by life or by death" (Phil. 1:20).

Commitment is an action

Commitment may begin with an attitude, but it does not end there. An attitude that goes no farther than our mind is nothing more than a good intention; it doesn't qualify as a commitment.

Real commitment produces results. We would all be in deep trouble if God's commitment to us had only produced the thought, perhaps even the desire, to send Christ to die on the cross for our sins. Our salvation took more than a plan; it took action. As noble as we might consider the intention, Jesus had to be born as a son and die as a sacrifice to purchase our salvation.

Commitment is costly, which is perhaps why we admire it so much in other people but prefer to avoid it ourselves.

When we entrust ourselves to someone or something, it might mean we have to give up something that we hold dear.

Some Christians, for example, have felt called of God to return to the inner city and win the forgotten and unloved to Christ. This requires an attitude of commitment, but it also requires sacrificial action. These people not only give up the comforts of suburbia for the rat- and cockroach-infested tenements, they put their families on the line. Their children face the same dangers of gang violence, the same temptations of easy drugs and the same limitations of the school system as any inner-city child does. The commitment of these people is not just a desire that impacts themselves; it's an action that affects the lives of their families.

If we say we have commitment, the world wants to see it. As James says in his epistle, "But someone will say, 'You have faith, and I have works.' Show me your faith without your works, and I will show you my faith by my works" (James 2:18). If you have a committed attitude, everyone is watching to see it in your actions.

The importance of commitment

Commitment that begins with an attitude and results in action forms an essential element in our society. It implies dependability. When we go to the hospital, we are depending on the commitment of the doctors and nurses to do their best to provide health care. When we send our children to school, we are depending on the commitment of the teachers and administration to keep our sons and daughters safe and to impart knowledge to them that will be of value later in life. When we cash our paycheck, we are depending on the commitment of the company we work for to have the money available to redeem those checks and, ultimately, that the government who issues those green slips of paper we receive from the bank has the resources to back up its commitment to the value printed on the paper.

The importance of commitment is seen throughout society. In fact, when commitment fails, society fails. The failure of quality in manufacturing is largely due to the failure of commitment to quality by companies and workers. The failure of banks and savings and loan institutions is frequently due to the failure of bank investors to make wise investments.

Governments rely on patriotism. That's commitment. Children rely on loving care from their parents. That's commitment. Parachurch ministries rely on the financial support of those who are blessed by them. That's commitment. Computer operators rely on support services for help when something goes wrong. That's commitment. When commitment dies, governments, families, ministries and businesses fail. Look around you and make your own assessment of the health of commitment in society today.

When commitment fails

The importance of commitment is evident by the negative consequences that result when we fail to follow through on our commitments. One of the most obvious is in the area of marriage. Divorce, at its simplest, is the result of one or both of the marriage partners reneging on their commitment. When they vowed before God and those who came to witness their ceremony that they would take one another "for better or for worse," they may not have realized how much worse it could get. Someone has quipped that marriages would be better off if, instead of taking each other for better or worse, couples took each other for good.

Marriage is supposed to be a commitment until death. Yet statistics show that only 51 percent of children today live with both biological parents. In 1994 there were 1.2 million divorces, of which 53 percent involved minor children.[1] That hurts! A writer to the letters column of the *Indianapolis Star* who had gone through a 'terrible divorce and custody battle" observed that "the real losers are the children and society. . . . Break the family foundation and society has no foundation."[2] The family foundation is built with the concrete of commitment.

Twenty years ago many Americans were concerned about the increase in divorce, but they were assured that the breakdown in the commitment between adults would have no lasting effect on the children. They were wrong. Children from single-parent families, whether through divorce or illegitimacy, are two to three times as likely to have emotional or behavioral problems, and half again as likely to have learning disabilities.[3] *U.S. News & World Report* cited a study that indicated 57 percent of state prison inmates grew up with one parent absent from the home. The study went on to say that a missing father, in particular, is a better predictor of criminal activity than race or poverty.[4]

Sociologists Sara McLanahan and Gary Sandefur say in their book, *Growing Up With a Single Parent*, that young women who were reared in disrupted families are twice as likely to become teen mothers. The absence of a father increases a child's likelihood of being a dropout, jobless, a drug addict, a suicide victim, mentally ill and a target of child sexual abuse.[5]

Those who would argue that marital commitment is nice but not a necessity need to rethink their position. In fact, the Bible says otherwise. God's wisdom, nearly 3,000 years ago, said, "Rejoice with the wife of your youth. As a loving deer and a graceful doe, let her breasts satisfy you at all times; and always be enraptured with her love" (Prov. 5:18–19).

It's time we pull our head out of this permissive society's sand and look around us. Common sense dictates the necessity for commitment if our society is to function properly. But we have more than common sense. We have God's guide to right choices. We need to be familiar with the guide and to follow it into choices that please God and preserve society.

Choosing commitments wisely

Some commitments are ours by virtue of where we were born. As one born in the United States, for example, I have a commitment to the U.S. government to the degree that it doesn't violate God's laws. If you were born and live in another country, your commitment is to the government of that nation. We also have commitments to parents and children and spouses, which come as the result of birth or marriage. But there are other commitments that we are free to choose or disregard. Usually it is these commitments for which we need God's wisdom.

A commitment to God

As strange as it may seem, a commitment to God is an option, not a requirement. God respects our individual rights. He does not force Himself upon anyone. Yet His wisdom reminds us that only fools say, "There is no God" (Ps. 14:1). Only a fool could look around him, see the marvels of nature and say, "I don't believe in God. This is all by chance."

Yet if there is a God, the Creator of us as well as everything else we see, then we by necessity must submit to that God and commit ourselves to serve Him. The relationship between what is created and the One creating it implies the need to submit to the Creator. This is certainly true of our Creator. One who is this great and powerful cannot wisely be ignored, nor can His claim of ownership wisely be denied.

I remember the time I chose to make that commitment. I was only five years old. My father pastored two churches in western Pennsylvania. One of these churches, the smaller of the two, invited a children's evangelist to come and hold services. It was in the dead of winter. One night during this series of meetings the evangelist said, "Even if your father was the pastor of this church, that would not save you. You need to trust Christ for yourself." This caught my attention because there were only two of us to whom that statement could apply— my older brother and me. My brother had already received Christ as his Savior, and that night I felt the Holy Spirit tugging at my heart. I went forward and, with the help of the evangelist, made my commitment to Jesus. It's a commitment I've never regretted.

God's wisdom says, "Forsake foolishness and live, and go in the way of understanding" (Prov. 9:6). Stop living like the fool who denies there is a God. Instead, recognize what your eyes and your heart both tell you and acknowledge the Lord. Proverbs 19:23 assures us, "The fear of the LORD leads to life, and he who has it will abide in satisfaction; he will not be visited with evil."

Such a commitment provides two important elements for our life: satisfaction and security.

Nothing in life seems to truly satisfy. Whatever we gain in a short time leaves us thirsting for more. History is strewn with examples. Alexander the Great was not satisfied, even when he had completely subdued the known nations of his day. He wept because there were no more worlds to conquer, and he died at an early age in a state of debauchery. Hannibal, who filled three bushels with the gold rings taken from the enemies he had slaughtered, committed suicide by swallowing poison. Few noted his passing, and he died completely unmourned. Julius Caesar conquered 800 cities and became the leader of one of the greatest earthly kingdoms ever, only to be stabbed by his best friends at the scene of his greatest triumph. Napoleon Bonaparte, after being the scourge of Europe, spent his last years in exile.

Each one of these men died empty, disappointed and disillusioned. But that doesn't have to be the case with you. Luke tells of a just and devout man named Simeon who came to the temple at the time Joseph and Mary brought the baby Jesus to be dedicated. Simeon "took Him up in his arms and blessed God and said: 'Lord, now You are letting Your servant depart in peace, according to Your word; for my eyes have seen Your salvation'" (Luke 2:28–30). These were the words of a satisfied man. Only Jesus can truly satisfy you.

Proverbs 19:23 also promises security. It says that he who fears the Lord "will not be visited with evil." That does not mean we will never be hurt or disappointed. People will still say and do wrong things that will hurt us. But as Warren Wiersbe, former director of Back to the Bible, is fond of saying, "They can hurt us but not harm us." Jesus said, "And do not fear those who kill the body but cannot kill the soul. But rather fear Him who is able to destroy both soul and body in hell" (Matt. 10:28). Only the fear of God can dispel the fear of men. When we fear God and make a commitment to His son, Jesus, we need never fear anything else.

A commitment to God's Word

The great statesman Daniel Webster held a high view of Scripture. He warned of the disastrous results if it were ignored: "If we abide by the principles taught in the Bible, our country will go on prospering, . . . but if we and our posterity neglect its instructions and authority, no man can tell how sudden a catastrophe may overwhelm us and bury all our glory in profound obscurity." Webster was talking about a commitment to God's Word that goes beyond believing that it is true. Many Christians agree that the Bible is the Word of God, and most would even say that the Bible is true. But despite these affirmations, they fail to apply it to their lives. They consider the Bible true, but not pertinent.

Someone has said, "The devil doesn't care what you believe about the Bible as long as you don't practice it." It's sad when the great treasure of God's Word remains an untouched, unread, unrealized book of theory. The Bible was not written to be theory; it was written to be practiced. God's wisdom says, "For the commandment is a lamp, and the law is light" (Prov. 6:23). A lamp is not made to look at but to provide light so people can see. A light is what God has given us to dispel spiritual darkness. The Bible is both of these.

When electricity was first introduced to the remote areas of Wales, a woman went to a great deal of trouble to have electrical power installed in her home. The electric company noticed, however, that she didn't seem to use much electricity. In fact, her usage was minuscule. So they sent a meter reader out to check on the matter. The man came to the door and said, "We've looked at the amount of electricity your meter says you use. It's so small that we were wondering if you use it." "Oh, yes," she said, "we use it. We turn it on every night to see how to light our lamps and then we switch it off again."

Before you think this woman foolish, remember that this is exactly the way many Christians use their Bible. They turn it on to follow their pastor's sermon on Sunday morning, and then turn it off the rest of the week. Chuck Colson reported that when 1,382 people were asked in a survey what book had most influenced their lives, only 15 cited the Bible—barely more than one percent.[6]

God gave us the Bible to guide our lives. Proverbs says, "The way of the righteous is made plain" (15:19, KJV). Our way is made plain in the Bible, but we still have to follow it.

Commitment to prayer

Martin Luther said, "If I should neglect prayer but a single day, I should lose a great deal of the fire of faith."[7] Many Christians go for days, if not weeks, without uttering a prayer more than a table grace at dinner time. No wonder we lack fire!

Mrs. Oswald Chambers once said of her husband, "Like all teachers of forceful personality, he constantly had people longing to pour out their intimate troubles to him. I remember at the close of one meeting a woman came up to him with the words, 'Oh, Mr. Chambers, I feel I must tell you about myself.' As he led her away to a quiet corner, I resigned myself to a long wait; but he was back again in a few minutes. As we went home, I remarked on the speed with which he managed to free himself, and he replied, 'I just asked her if she had ever told God all about herself. When she said she hadn't, I advised her to go home and pour out before Him as honestly as she could all her troubles, then see if she still needed or wanted to relate them to me.'" There is nothing wrong with sharing our burdens with our brothers or sisters in Christ, but our first commitment is to share them with God.

Provers 15:8 says, "The sacrifice of the wicked is an abomination to the LORD, *but the prayer of the upright is His delight*" (italics mine). Do you want to delight God? Do you want to please Him? Then make a commitment to pray. That's how you spend intimate time with Him. Commit yourself to fervent prayer. James says, "The effective, fervent prayer of a righteous man avails much" (James 5:16).

Memorial Stadium, where the Nebraska Cornhuskers play football, is located on the west side of Lincoln. As far as 56 blocks away (about three quarters of the way across town), one can easily hear the enthusiastic roar of the 76,000 fans as they cheer on their team. While I'm not suggesting you disturb your neighbors across the street, I would encourage some of the same energy and sincerity that we demonstrate at football games to be shown in your prayers. Insipid praying is not pleasing to God. He does not delight in the rote recitation of prayer terminology worn bare by frequent usage. God wants prayers that ring with the conviction of truth, that are fortified with the faith that He is the only answer, that resound with enthusiasm for an omnipotent, omniscience, omnipresent God. When we pray like that, God is eager to hear us (see 2 Kings 19:15–19, 35–37).

Commit yourself also to consistent prayer. God does not always answer right away. Sometimes He tests us or gives us time to rethink the appropriateness of our requests. But at the right time, in the time He wills, the answer will come. In the meantime, keep on praying. Don't quit. Remember Jesus' story about the man who went to borrow bread late at night from his neighbor (Luke 11:5-10). Persistence pays. Keep on asking, keep on seeking, keep on knocking on heaven's door. It's always too soon to give up!

Martin Luther recalled an occasion when his puppy came to the table looking for a morsel from his master. The little dog watched with open mouth and motionless eyes, waiting for a tidbit to be tossed his way. Luther said, "Oh, if I could only pray the way this dog watches the meat! All of his thoughts are concentrated on the piece of meat. Otherwise he has no thought, wish or hope."[8] Too frequently we give up praying just before God sends His answer. The disciples said that they were going to give themselves "continually to prayer" (Acts 6:4). We should as well.

Commitment to forgiveness

Robert Louis Stevenson wrote of two unmarried sisters who had such a bitter ruckus they stopped speaking to each other. Unable or unwilling to leave their small home, they continued to use the same rooms and sleep in the same bedroom. A chalk line divided the sleeping area into two halves, separating doorway and fireplace, so that each could come and go and get her own meals without trespassing on her sister's domain. In the night they could hear each other breathe. For years they coexisted in grinding silence. Neither was willing to take the first step to reconciliation.[9] What an unhappy way to live. Yet it happens too often, even among Christians. Someone has said that bitterness or unforgivingness may be the most common sin among Christians.

This is not a new experience among those who call themselves Christians. History tells us that Michelangelo, the sculptor, and Raphael, the painter, were both commissioned to do works of art for the beautification of the Vatican. Although each had a different job and both were highly respected, there arose such a bitter spirit of rivalry between them that at last they would not even speak when they met. Their jealous attitude toward one another was obvious to everyone. The saddest aspect of their feud was that both were supposed to be doing their work "for the glory of God."

Who hasn't felt a twinge of satisfaction when we have heard that someone who has hurt us has experienced misfortune himself. We may not openly admit it, but a small voice within us says, "Well, they finally got what they deserved." We might even think, *God has vindicated me at last.* In truth, however, the problem is not with God but with us. God is too big to feel a need to get even with someone; we aren't. That's why God's wisdom says, "Do not rejoice when your enemy falls, and do not let your heart be glad when he stumbles; lest the LORD see it, and it displease Him" (Prov. 24:17-18).

Take God's warning seriously. Proverbs 17:5 admonishes, "He who is glad at calamity will not go unpunished." When we refuse to forgive someone, we lay up a store of misfortune for ourselves.

Bitterness eats away at our body. In his book *None of These Diseases*, Dr. S. I. McMillen describes how physical maladies, including ulcers, high blood pressure and strokes, are connected to harboring resentment and hatred toward others. He says, "It might be written on many thousands of death certificates that the victim died of 'grudgitis.'"[10]

Failure to forgive affects our mental processes as well. C. S. Lewis wrote in his *Letters to an American Lady*, "The greatest evil nasty people can do to us is to become an obsession with us."[11] When we allow a root of unforgivingness to bring forth bitterness, we become a slave to the person we hate. We will avoid going places or break off relationships with others, not because we want to, but because of the effect that bitterness has upon us. The person we hate may live miles away; they may even be dead, yet they control our lives.

Perhaps worst of all, unforgivingness destroys our relationship with the Lord. The Lord's Prayer says, "And forgive us our debts, as we forgive our debtors" (Matt. 6:12). Failure to forgive is a sin. As long as we harbor this sin in our heart, God can't forgive us. When we have unconfessed sin in our lives, it prevents us from relating fully to God and eventually damages our spiritual lives.

That's a high price to pay for the privilege of destroying your body, mind and soul. Why live as a drudge to a grudge when you can forgive and really live.

Commitment to compassion

"Compassion fatigue" is a new term heard among some people of our affluent society today. It means, "I'm tired of repeated calls to do good." Some wealthy people are beginning to ask, "Why must my enjoyment of the good life be spoiled by reminders that most of the world is slowly starving and many of our own neighborhoods are terribly poor? Our superhighways and city shelters help keep these people out of sight. Why can't I ignore them as well?"

We are often like the man who was telling his wife about passing a woman in a downpour of rain one afternoon. She had a flat tire and was standing helplessly by the side of her car. He said, "I thought to myself how awful it is of people not to help such a poor woman. I would have stopped if I were not on my way to work."

Proverbs 17:5 provides the answer: "He who mocks the poor reproaches his Maker." In other words, poor people were made as much in the image of God as rich people. When we slight the poor, we are also showing disrespect toward the God whose image they bear. That is why Jesus said, "Assuredly, I say to you, inasmuch as you did it to one of the least of these My brethren, you did it to Me" (Matt. 25:40).

One night in 1935, Fiorello H. La Guardia, a former mayor of New York City, showed up at a night court in the poorest ward of the city. He dismissed the judge for the evening and took over the bench. One case involved an elderly woman who was caught stealing bread to feed her grandchildren. La Guardia said, "I've got to punish you. Ten dollars or ten days in jail."

As he spoke, he threw $10 into his hat. He then fined everyone in the courtroom 50 cents for living in a city "where a person has to steal bread so that her grandchildren can eat." The hat was passed around, and the woman left the courtroom with her fine paid and an additional $47.50.

On television we see pictures of starving children in Africa and India, homeless people sleeping on top of heating grates in big cities, devastated homes of tornado victims, and we feel overwhelmed. Yet God does not call us as individuals to care for the world. He simply asks us to show compassion for those in need whom He lays upon our hearts, and there are plenty of those. God asks that a neighbor help his neighbors, that a Christian brother help his Christian brothers.

It's good to pray for the needs of the world, but don't close your eyes too long. If you do, dozens of needy people will cross your path and you will never see them, let alone help them. Open your eyes to the needy around you. Choose one family to help or one person to help. If each of us does a little, together we can do a lot.

A call to commitment

In *The Frog in the Kettle: What Christians Need to Know About Life in the Year 2000*, George Barna says that the willingness to make a commitment is failing fast. He writes, "Commitment is viewed negatively because it limits our ability to feel independent and free, to experience new things, to change our minds on the spur of the moment and to focus upon self-gratification rather than helping others."[12]

The wisdom of the world says, "Don't be a chump. Commitments are for losers. Keep your options open." But God's wisdom says, "A faithful man will abound with blessings" (Prov. 28:20). Don't allow the fact that others lack commitment rob you of the blessings of faithfulness.

When Moses said, "Whoever is on the LORD's side, let him come to me" (Ex. 32:26), it was a call to commitment. When Elijah asked, "How long will you falter between two opinions? If the LORD is God, follow Him" (1 Kings 18:21), it was a call to commitment. When Jesus said, "If anyone desires to come after Me, let him deny himself, and take up his cross, and follow Me" (Matt. 16:24), it was a call to commitment.

Do you hear God's call for greater commitment in your life? Do you have your spiritual antennae up, ready to hear God when He asks you to follow Him? When you hear Him, do you obey? At what level of commitment to God, to His Word, to His will do you live today? The comfort of commitment is the greatest comfort of all. Enjoy it all the days of your life.

[1] *U.S. News & World Report*, February 27, 1995, p. 39.

[2] Mark Snare, "Marriage breakup," *Indianapolis Star*, May 25, 1995, p. A11.

[3] Lee Smith, "The New Wave of Illegitimacy," *Fortune*, April 18, 1994, p. 82.

[4] *U.S. News & World Report*, February 27, 1995, p. 39.

[5] Ibid.

[6] Charles Colson, *Who Speaks for God?* (Westchester, Ill.: Crossway Books, 1985), p. 88.

[7] Martin Luther, *Luther's Tabletalk*, quoted in *Tabletalk*, Vol. 11, No. 1, February 1987.

[8] Ibid.

[9] Robert Louis Stevenson, "Edinburgh: Picturesque Notes," *The Works of Robert Louis Stevenson, Vol. 3* (New York: Peter Fenelon Collier), p. 42.

[10] Dr. S. I. McMillen, *None of These Diseases* (Westwood, N.J.: Fleming H. Revell Co., 1963), p. 71.

[11] C. S. Lewis, *Letters to an American Lady* (Grand Rapids, Mich.: Eerdmans, 1967), p. 27.

[12] George Barna, *The Frog in the Kettle* (Ventura, Calif.: Regal Books, 1990), p. 35.

Conclusion

The key theme of Proverbs is wisdom, and it occurs again and again throughout the book. But the wisdom found in Proverbs is not just any wisdom— it is God's wisdom. There is worldly wisdom, such as the kind we find in pop psychology and paperback how-to books. But this is often simply foolishness based on temporary fads and passing fancies. It more often evades reality than confronts it. It is more concerned with finding the easy and "miraculous" way to deal with the issues of life. This kind of wisdom produces grapefruit diets and snake oil remedies.

There is also secular wisdom, which is often found in scientific or academic settings. This wisdom may be more factual but offers no better solutions. It is knowledge without the ability to beneficially apply what it knows.

God's wisdom, on the other hand, is always related to His will and His way: Because God is eternal, His wisdom is timeless as well. His truths never lose their value and never go out of date. God's wisdom is not only based on facts, it is forever relevant. His wisdom says:

"A wise man will hear and increase learning, and a man of understanding will attain wise counsel, to understand a proverb and an enigma, the words of the wise and their riddles. The fear of the LORD is the beginning of knowledge" (Prov. 1:5-7).

"For the LORD gives wisdom; from His mouth come knowledge and understanding" (Prov. 2:6).

"When wisdom enters your heart, and knowledge is pleasant to your soul, discretion will preserve you; understanding will keep you, to deliver you from the way of evil, from the man who speaks perverse things" (Prov. 2:10-12).

"Happy is the man who finds wisdom, and the man who gains understanding; for her proceeds are better than the profits of silver, and her gain than fine gold" (Prov. 3:13–14).

"For the ways of man are before the eyes of the LORD, and He ponders all his paths" (Prov. 5:21).

"The fear of the LORD is the beginning of wisdom, and the knowledge of the Holy One is understanding" (Prov. 9:10).

"In the way of righteousness is life, and in its pathway there is no death" (Prov. 12:28).

"There is a way which seems right to a man, but its end is the way of death" (Prov. 14:12).

As we study the Book of Proverbs, we find that these themes fall into a pattern. We discover that God's wisdom stands behind God's will; God's will stands behind God's way; and God's way stands behind our well-being.

Action steps

If we want God's wisdom to be a part of our lives, we need to take the following seven action steps:

1. Determine to set a time and a place where every day you will seek wisdom from God's Word.

The well-known man of faith George Mueller admitted that the first three years after his conversion he negelected the Word of God. When he began to search it diligently, he found that overflowing blessings came from his daily study. Mueller considered the day unprofitable when he did not have a good time over the Word of God.

Admittedly, a consistent time in the Word is one of the biggest hurdles Christians face, whether they are new believers or have lived the Christian life for many years. Our busy schedules keep trying to press this important time out of our lives.

The best approach is to treat your time with the Lord just like you would any other appointment. Don't expect to find time—you will have to make it. Set it for a time of day when you are least likely to have interruptions. For many people that means getting up earlier in the morning. Set it for a time when you are at your best. If you aren't an early morning person, you might need to take a mid-morning break and instead of consuming a candy bar and can of soda, spend the time ingesting the Word of God.

Pick a place that you can identify with your time with the Lord. Your bed, for example, would probably not make a good place since it is identified with sleep and that's probably what will happen if you try to spend time with the Lord there. A chair with an end table for your Bible and other items you may want to use makes an excellent choice.

2. Make yourself accountable to a spouse or other wisdom-seeking friend.

Ultimately, we are accountable to God, but since He is invisible and doesn't speak with an audible voice, it's easy to excuse, ignore or otherwise rationalize away any obligation we might have to meet with Him. That's why it often helps if we are also accountable to a fellow wisdom-seeking friend.

3. Record your spiritual discoveries.

Every Christian who has grown head and shoulders above the Christians around him has kept some form of spiritual diary. Many of them, such as *The Diary of David Brainard* and *The Journals of John Wesley*, are good reading and could be included in your devotional time. Whether yours ever become published or not, it still makes good spiritual sense to keep track of what God has said to you through the Scriptures.

We are all better at forgetting than remembering. Precious truths and insights may be lost to us if we rely on our memory. Furthermore, these journals become a source of encouragement as we look back through their pages and see the faithfulness of God. Some people who keep journals make it a tradition to reread the previous year's notes as they enter the new year. The confidence of "God with us" can jump-start us for the year ahead.

4. Search for God's answers before you get the world's questions.

The motto "Always be prepared" didn't originate with the Boy Scouts; it came from the Bible. The apostle Peter says, "Always be ready to give a defense to everyone who asks you a reason for the hope that is in you" (1 Pet. 3:15). Many people live by worldly wisdom and find it foolish. They then search secular wisdom and find it inadequate. Now they want to try God's wisdom. Will you be prepared to explain it to them?

None of us knows the Bible so thoroughly that we have all the answers; but the better we know the Bible, the more answers we will have. Take note of the answers that God's Word gives on such issues as, "Why are we here?" "Where are we going?" "How am I supposed to live?" Neither worldly wisdom nor secular wisdom can answer these questions— but God's wisdom can.

5. Ask God to help you apply His wisdom to your ways.

The writers of the Bible were inspired by the Holy Spirit as they wrote. Second Peter 1:21 says, "For prophecy never came by the will of man, but holy men of God spoke as they were moved by the Holy Spirit." Just as Scripture was inspired by the Spirit, we need that selfsame Holy Spirit to apply it to our lives. To think that we can use human wisdom to understand and appropriate God's wisdom places us in the same position as the Christians at Galatia, whom Paul admonished, "Having begun in the Spirit, are you now being made perfect by the flesh?" (Gal. 3:3).

Before you open God's Word, take a moment to ask Him to open your eyes to the truths you need for your life. This is also an appropriate time to confess any known sin that might hinder the Spirit's work in your heart. Claim God's promise found in John 16:13 that "He will guide you into all truth."

6. Don't get discouraged.

Always remember, if it were easy, more people would do it. The fact that you chose to read this book indicates that you desire spiritual growth. If you don't find the answers right away, keep looking. Jesus said, "Ask, and it will be given to you; seek, and you will find; knock, and it will be opened to you" (Matt. 7:7). Literally, He said, "Keep on seeking."

In addition, don't be afraid to ask for help from others who appear to have a healthy spiritual life. Someone once compared understanding the Bible to three men trying to climb an 18-foot wall. By themselves, none could do it, but when they stood on each other's shoulders, the top man could climb over and then help the other two as well. We all stand on the shoulders of godly men of the past.

One caution, however, is that you should never take anyone else's understanding of Scripture at face value. Always go back to the Word to see if there are any contradictions. Luke praised the Christians at Berea because they "searched the Scriptures daily to find out whether these things were so" (Acts 17:11).

Also, remember that the Christian life is not a sprint but a lifelong marathon. No matter how many years you spend reading the Bible, you will discover new truths and new wisdom each time you search its pages. Relax and enjoy the journey. Your time in the Word is to be a delight, not a burden. Don't be afraid to say, "I don't know, but I know where the answer can be found."

7. Don't wait.

There is truth in the old adage, "The road to hell is paved with good intentions." As born-again Christians, we may not have to worry about hell, but we do need to be concerned about our spiritual growth. You will never see much spiritual growth in your life unless you determine to make a regular intake of God's Word a priority in your Christian walk. The longer you wait, the more opportunity Satan has to bring situations into your life that can cause serious damage. Furthermore, as you procrastinate, you lose opportunities to store up for yourself treasures in heaven (Matt. 6:20). In essence, you lose all the way around. Determine that you will not wait another day, but right now, you will do whatever is necessary to start seeking God's wisdom for your life.

Shoe-leather Christianity

Nobody can claim to have God's wisdom until it affects the way he lives. Having wisdom in your head is no substitute for having it in your shoes. Proverbs 14:16 says, "A wise man fears and *departs* from evil, but a fool rages and is self-confident" (italics mine).

Proverbs is God's guide to life's choices. It will give you insight both in how to go to heaven when you die and how to live peacefully and prosperously in the Lord until you die. Read it again and again. Don't allow its inestimable value to get by you. God's Word is where you learn God's wisdom; if you are determined to live wisely, then turn back to the Bible.